# IMAGES OF
# Rural Britain

# IMAGES OF
# Rural Britain

## CHRISTOPHER SOMERVILLE

PHOTOGRAPHY BY SWIFT IMAGERY

FOREWORD BY BARONESS YOUNG OF OLD SCONE

NEW HOLLAND

First published in 2001 by New Holland Publishers (UK) Ltd
London • Cape Town • Sydney • Auckland

10 9 8 7 6 5 4 3 2 1

86–88 Edgware Road, London W2 2EA, United Kingdom
Website: www.newhollandpublishers.com

80 McKenzie Street, Cape Town 8001, South Africa

14 Aquatic Drive, Frenchs Forest, NSW 2086, Australia

218 Lake Road, Northcote, Auckland, New Zealand

Hardback ISBN  1 85974 880 5
Paperback ISBN  1 85974 627 6

Publishing Manager: Jo Hemmings
Project Editor: Mike Unwin
Copy Editor: Sue Viccars
Assistant Editor: Camilla MacWhannell
Designer & Cover Design: Harry Green
Production: Joan Woodroffe

Reproduction by Pica Digital Pte Ltd, Singapore

Printed and bound in Singapore by Kyodo Printing Co
(Singapore) Pte Ltd

**DEDICATION**
For my parents John and Elizabeth Somerville

PAGE 1  A handloom weaver
at Kingston St Mary,
Somerset, keeps alive the
tradition of rural crafts.

PAGE 2  There are no cars in
Clovelly – the cobbled main
street of the most picturesque
village on the north Devon
coast is too steep. Donkeys
do the donkey work,
transporting the luggage of
guests up and down between
the New Inn and the car park
on the cliffs above.

PAGE 5  Bluebells carpet the
floor of a wood at Wrington
Hill, north Somerset.

PAGES 6–7
(CLOCKWISE FROM TOP LEFT)
Gertrude Jekyll designed
the gardens of Abbotswood
House at Lower Swell in the
Cotswolds.

Traditional farming with horse
and handplough in Somerset.

The princely façade of
Blenheim Palace overshadows
a local cricket match.

The placid River Stour winds
through Dedham Vale on the
borders of Suffolk and Essex,
countryside immortalised in
the landscape paintings of
John Constable.

Medieval timber framing
supports the lath-and-plaster
walls of the oldest cottage in
Eardisland, Herefordshire.

The twin towers of Truro's
neo-Gothic cathedral
dominate the southern
Cornish landscape for
miles around.

PAGE 9  Early-morning mist
invests a boathouse on
Ullswater in the Lake District
with the dreaminess of a
Japanese painting.

# FOREWORD

he variety of the built and natural heritage of rural Britain is rich and fascinating, both telling the story of the history that shaped our rural settlements, buildings and landscapes and uplifting the spirit with their charm and beauty.

Whole landscapes are redolent with a sense of the people who lived there and their close dependence on the natural rhythms and resources of the countryside around them. The very shape of our distinctive natural areas of Britain has been determined by the land uses which formed them over the past thousands of years. People, landscape and the habitats on which our wildlife depend are intimately linked.

Even today, when the majority of people live in the towns and cities and many may rarely go to the countryside, the concern felt for the unique qualities of rural landscapes and habitats still figures high. A recent opinion poll indicated that the countryside was the second most valued aspect of life in Britain after freedom of speech.

The increased opportunity for access to the countryside brought about by the Countryside and Rights of Way Act will, I hope, encourage many others to visit the countryside and enjoy its built and natural heritage.

Of course, the British countryside is one of our most valuable tourist assets. Diversification in the agricultural industry is increasing the range of opportunities for rural tourism, allowing more people to enjoy the distinctive character of more country places and this has been helped further by National Lottery investment. Further agricultural reform is essential to reward land farmers for providing public benefits such as conservation and access.

This stunning book captures the visual and cultural splendour of the wide variety of the British countryside. I am sure it will encourage still more people to enjoy the heritage of the countryside and to join in ensuring that it is properly protected and valued for the future.

BARONESS YOUNG OF OLD SCONE
*Chief Executive of the Environment Agency*

# 1

# LEAVING LONDON

## THE SMOOTH ATTRACTIONS
## OF THE HOME COUNTIES

ABOVE: Hughenden Manor was the country house of Benjamin Disraeli from 1847 until his death in 1881. The one-time prime minister lies buried in Hughenden churchyard; the church contains a fine memorial to him, erected at the wishes of Queen Victoria.

OPPOSITE: The Thames flows down to London past Cookham in Berkshire, one of the river's most appealing stretches.

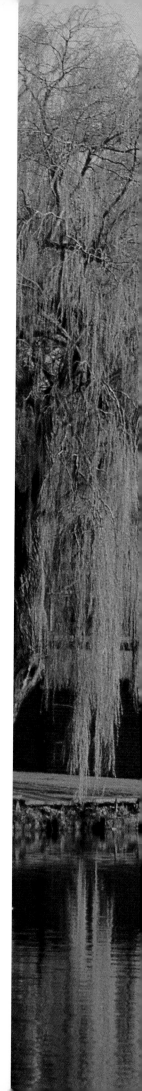

A S ORBITAL MOTORWAYS GO, the M25 is not a thing of beauty. Three parallel lanes of nose-to-tail traffic with attendant noise and fumes do not pose much of an enticement to linger along the 120-mile (193-kilometre) circle of tarmac that corsets London. But one virtue the M25 does possess. Looking outward as you crawl round its perimeter, you enjoy a grandstand view unrolling over the ring of glorious countryside encircling Britain's capital city.

Chalk and sand underlie this gently rolling landscape, giving it a sense of light and warmth. Beech and oak woods flourish. There is more horse-riding for pleasure here than anywhere else in Britain. Villages lie snug in mellow brick under thatch or red roof tiles; parish churches are beautifully maintained; cottage gardens are immaculately manicured. The lawns of large country houses (thick on the ground hereabouts) are kept pin-tidy. Well-heeled commuters inhabit them: stockbrokers, bankers, money men, media stars. The hand of wealth stretches protectively over the village greens, the broad acres, the jealously preserved woods and commons. This is London's own back garden, a charmed inner circle of counties – Surrey, Berkshire, Buckinghamshire, Hertfordshire – known collectively as the Home Counties, a title rich in smug regional chauvinism that conveys the sheltered and intimate nature of their relationship with the city.

London's own river approaches the capital in a succession of wide loops through the western Home Counties, forming the county boundary between Berkshire and Oxfordshire, and then the boundary between Berkshire and Buckinghamshire. This is the Thames's most appealing stretch, winding down to London under overhanging beech and willow between flat green meadows and softly rising hills clothed with woods that are famously beautiful in autumn. Here are the tall old watermills and sluice gates tucked away in backwaters that Ernest Shepard (1879–1976) loved to paint. Shepard used these Thames scenes as inspiration for his celebrated illustrations in *The Wind in the Willows*, the famous children's tale written by Kenneth Grahame (1859–1932). Grahame, a local resident while he was writing his book in the early 1900s, had the wooded banks of the Thames near Marlow in mind when he was creating the dreaded Wild Wood and other settings for the adventures of Mole, Rat, Badger and Mr Toad.

Other artists and writers have loved and celebrated this blend of water, open sky, meadow, woodland and hill. The 1889 comic classic *Three Men in a Boat*, written by Jerome K. Jerome (1859–1927), explored the Thames far upriver into Oxfordshire, while at Cookham in a Berkshire loop of the river lived and worked the wonderfully eccentric painter Stanley Spencer (1891–1959). Some of his large, locally set pictures

of the M25 and the western rim of London. Back in 1880 the City of London Corporation bought these 600 acres (250 hectares) of what the poet Thomas Gray (1716–1771) had called 'most venerable beeches, dreaming out their old stories to the wind'. It was an era of quick mass building, of headlong destruction of the remaining woodlands around London – most of these, as in the case of Burnham Beeches, terribly neglected. Nowadays the old forest is carefully looked after, safeguarded against any kind of encroachment or development, and threaded with dozens of well-used footpaths.

The towns along the river – Goring, Pangbourne, Henley, Marlow, Windsor – are as pretty as they are well-heeled. Henley has a handsome water frontage looking down on the scene of the annual Henley Royal Regatta – all champagne and upper-crust high jinks – while Windsor, of course, boasts the ultimate in eye-catching landmarks, Windsor Castle. The castle, London residence of the monarch when not at Buckingham Palace, dominates the view from all quarters with its great 12th-century Round Tower and cluster of turrets and battlemented walls. Stretching away south lies Windsor Great Park, 5,000 acres (2,000 hectares) of open grassland, trees and rides, crisscrossed with footpaths.

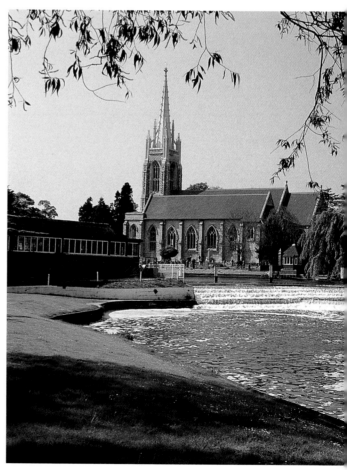

ABOVE: 'Most venerable beeches,' wrote the poet Thomas Gray of the ancient trees at Burnham Beeches, Buckinghamshire, 'dreaming out their old stories to the winds.'

RIGHT: The 180-mile (290-km) Thames Path National Trail runs past Marlow's river frontage en route to London, and gives excellent views of the town and its handsome church.

(*Christ Preaching at Cookham Regatta* and *Listening from Punts* among others) are displayed in the Stanley Spencer Gallery, a converted chapel at the bottom of Cookham High Street.

Set in the countryside around this stretch of the Thames are several very fine historic houses. Mapledurham near Pangbourne is a beautiful Tudor house beside the river, while the grand Victorian mansion of Cliveden – where Lord and Lady Astor ruled the ultra-smart 'Cliveden Set' of politicians and celebrities between the wars – looks across the Thames towards Cookham.

East of Cliveden, the ancient beech woods known as Burnham Beeches form a leafy buffer between the exclusive Thames-side country and the grittier purlieus

Alongside the Great Park, the Thames gives a wriggle around Magna Carta Island, a slip of mid-river land honoured by the British as the spot where in June 1215 King John was forced by his own barons to put his signature to the world's first charter of civil rights. From here the river winds on east into the outskirts of the capital.

The countryside north of the Thames is dominated by the rise of Londoners' favourite hill range, the Chiltern Hills. The Chilterns form a solid arc of sand, clay and chalk 30 miles (50 kilometres) long and about 15 miles (25 kilometres) wide, much of it clothed in short rabbit-nibbled turf and thick beech woods. The hills climb from the valley of the Thames between Goring and Windsor to sweep north-east in a great curved rampart, its outer face looking steeply down over the clay farmlands of Oxfordshire, Buckinghamshire and Bedfordshire. The Chilterns make wonderful walking country, high and airy for miles at a stretch, shadowy and secluded among the beech and oaks. Villages are tucked away along narrow lanes in the valleys that intersect the hills. Londoners coming out for a breath of spring air or an autumn ramble in the Chiltern Hills can scarcely believe that the city lies only just out of sight beyond the reverse slope of the landscape.

Trying to pick the prettiest corners of the Chilterns is like trying to select the sweetest in a punnet of prime

ABOVE: The circular 133-mile (214-km) Chiltern Way, devised as a Millennium Project by the Chiltern Society and opened in 2000, gives wonderful walking with grandstand views over the hills and beech woods.

LEFT: An exciting catwalk crosses the Thames at Hambleden Weir to reach the weatherboarded old mill, which ceased grinding corn in 1958 and was converted into flats. They command high prices, and some of the best views on the river.

OPPOSITE TOP: Butter wouldn't melt in its mouth these days, but West Wycombe was the scene of 18th-century Hellfire Club orgies.

OPPOSITE BOTTOM: Aldbury, a classically pretty Chiltern village where the architectural styles of many centuries live harmoniously side by side.

strawberries. But Hambleden – maybe because of its proximity to the Thames just north of Henley, and also thanks to its ease of access from London – is certainly one of the best loved. Hambleden is such a pearl of a place that the National Trust owns and maintains it. Shop, pub, church and charming roses-round-the-door cottages of brick and flint surround the village green. The pub, the Stag & Huntsman, looks a picture. So does St Mary's Church, a beautiful medieval building whose south chapel altar features intricate wood-carving from the 14th century. Also in St Mary's are the oak chest used in the Crimea by Lord Cardigan of Hambleden Manor (he commanded the Charge of the Light Brigade in 1854), and the curiously carved Saxon font in which he was baptised as a baby. On the hill slopes beyond, Great Wood leans over the delectable village.

North around the Chiltern curve lies West Wycombe, another village looked after by the National Trust. Among the fine old buildings that line the High Street is the half-timbered Church Loft, where in medieval times the churchwardens held their meetings. Felons cooled their heels in the cramped little prison cell built into the side of the archway, and travellers would kneel to pray publicly under a crucifix set in the outside wall. The niche is still there, and below it the stone has been worn hollow by countless penitent knees.

In parkland just outside the village stands West Wycombe House, built around 1700 for the Dashwood family. It was Sir Francis Dashwood whose rakehell lifestyle in Georgian times scandalised and delighted the neighbourhood. Dashwood was actually a bright man of wide-ranging tastes and interests; he produced a Prayer Book for 'young and lively people', and was knowledge-able about European art and architecture. But he was also a man with too much time and money on his hands. The politicians, peers and fast-living bucks he invited to join his notorious Hellfire Club were much the same sort of people. Together they held wild parties in the quarry caverns above the village, from which emanated tales of orgiastic sex sessions and Black Magic ritual. It was Sir Francis Dashwood who rebuilt the Church of St Lawrence on the hill overlooking West Wycombe, top-ping off the tower with a hollow golden globe in which he and his friends would drink and gamble in privacy. The big hexagonal mausoleum built by Dashwood on the slope below the church contains a number of stone urns in which the hearts of Hellfire Club members were supposed to be deposited. Enfolded in the Chiltern trees, these alleged hot spots seem innocent enough today.

Further north towards the outer edge of the Chilterns is Aldbury, everybody's idea of a chocolate-box-pretty English village with tree-fringed green and a

Tudor manor house admiring its own reflection in the duck pond. In the Church of St John the Baptist lie the richly carved 15th-century effigies of Sir Robert and Lady Whittingham, Sir Robert resting his feet on an ivy-girdled and hairy wild man of the woods. Up behind the village are the beech and pine woods of the Ashridge Estate, once owned by a man who despoiled more British countryside than most: the 3rd Duke of Bridgewater (1736–1803), pioneering sponsor of canal-building in this country. A 100-foot (30-metre) Doric column in a woodland clearing carries an inscription describing him as 'Father of Inland Navigation', but paternity of the infant transport system of the Industrial Revolution was shared with a humbler and probably more capable partner, the illiterate engineering genius James Brindley. The vast Gothic mansion of Ashridge House, 1,000 feet (300 metres) wide, squats on the next ridge.

Two of the most charming Chiltern villages have notable connections with the arts. George Bernard Shaw (1856–1950), the Irish Nobel Laureate playwright and polemicist, came to live at Ayot St Lawrence in the eastern Chilterns in 1906, aged 50, reputedly in hopes of enjoying a long life after he had read the phrase 'her time was short' on the tombstone of an Ayot woman who had died at an advanced age. The village air must have had some amaranthine quality to it, for Shaw lived at Ayot in full vigour for another 44 years. The village boasts one of the most picturesque and enjoyable pubs in Britain, the Brocket Arms, low-ceilinged, dark, lined with Tudor beams and cheerfully firelit.

A fire glows at Much Hadham, too, but this is the blacksmith's forge furnace where traditional smithing of ornamental and practical ironwork still goes on. Much Hadham, out on the easternmost fringe of the Chilterns, is a gem of a village, tucked down in the valley of the River Ash. Along the main street Tudor, Stuart, Georgian and Victorian buildings lean companionably together. St Andrew's Church contains some marvellous examples of the medieval stone-mason's skill, especially on the corbels high up in the nave walls: a gallant soldier, a king, a spinster, a scattering of demonic beasts. Outside, the west door is flanked by a pair of modern sculptures, the delicately modelled heads of a king and queen. They were carved and presented to the church by the master sculptor Henry Moore (1898–1986), who lived and worked until his death in the hamlet of Perry Green on the ridge a couple of miles away. Enigmatic recumbent figures, huge and smooth as whales, lie in the fields around the sculptor's house and studio.

Notwithstanding the charms of the Buckinghamshire and Hertfordshire villages, however, it is the countryside that makes the Chilterns. Those great beechwood forests stand proud on the chalk ridges with their characteristic rounded shape. In between are open grass slopes, rich in herbs and wild flowers, orchids, vetches, thyme, rockrose, marjoram, knapweed. A dense skein of footpaths and bridleways threads the open downland and the woods. The plunge from the Chiltern heights to the Oxfordshire and Bedfordshire plains is nowhere more than a few hundred feet; but the escarpment seems a mighty wall, never more so than from the ramparts of the Iron Age hill-fort on Ivinghoe Beacon. Here, at 755 feet (230 metres), the view north and east over the lower-lying pastures and cornlands is immense.

It is a view that has changed entirely in detail but hardly at all in broad-brush since Bronze Age travellers gazed out on it from the ridge 4,000 years ago. They would have been following the great old cross-Britain

trackway that changes name from Ridgeway to Icknield Way and then to Peddar's Way as it runs east towards the East Anglian flatlands. To Ivinghoe Beacon comes the Ridgeway, deeply rutted, broad and chalky, at the end of a 90-mile (145-kilometre) run from the stone circle at Avebury, down in Wiltshire. From the Beacon it leaves as the Icknield Way, aiming for Suffolk 100 miles (161 kilometres) off, a journey along the sides of hills and shallow valleys. People have trodden this high and mighty trackway for time out of mind – perhaps 6,000 or 7,000 years. They still do, though nowadays off-road sports vehicles, heavy agricultural tyre treads, the shoes of horses and the hooves of cows all vie with the cleated boot soles of walkers to turn the surface of the Ridgeway/Icknield Way into a dour, sucking porridge. Trudging the old track 'on a

ABOVE: By the 1970s, after centuries of persecution by farmers and gamekeepers, the red kite was considered one of the most endangered of British bird species. But the recent reintroduction to the Chilterns of these handsome birds of prey with their characteristic forked tails has been a resounding success, with the population soaring to well over 300 by the turn of the 21st century.

shoeful of blisters' in the summer of 1911, the supreme country writer Edward Thomas (1878–1917), so soon to blossom into an even more sublime poet, came striding up Telegraph Hill. In the book he wrote about his long walk, *The Icknield Way*, he described how he found the track spattered with daisies and hung with roses. On arrival at the Beacon early on a hot, misty morning, he 'saw Ivinghoe Church tower and the silly spire, short and sharp, on top of it, the misty woods behind the Pitstone Church tower and an elm throned on a rise together, and the broad wooded valley beyond. Larks sang ...'

There is a great buttress of tree-blanketed downland south of London, too: the chalk and greensand arc of the North Downs that sweeps east from Surrey into Kent. Beeches do well, of course; also oaks and twisty hornbeams. These woods, unlike the light and leisurely beech hangers of the Chilterns, were serious industrial workplaces, stinking with smoke and ringing with noise when the medieval iron-smelting trade was in full swing. Deep in the Abinger woods lie the hammer ponds whose out-rushing sluice water turned wheels that drove the great trip hammers of the ironmasters. These days the ponds are miniature ecosystems given over to nature, haunted by frogs and dragonflies. The woods themselves, in no danger nowadays of being cut down for charcoal or cleared for agriculture, are crossed by networks of well-used footpaths.

Hemmed in by trees at 965 feet (294 metres), Leith Hill is the highest point in the county of Surrey, and you can scramble up the 18th-century tower there (the builder, Richard Hull, lies buried under the floor) to get even higher. The view over trees and farmland is immense, with glimpses of London to the north. A viewpoint and beauty spot better known among Londoners is Box Hill, an open vantage point a few miles to the north on the brow of the North Downs at just under 600 feet (172 metres). It's a stiff climb up from the River Mole, ascending through groves of wild box trees and yews. Reward is at the top, a great view south into Kent that thousands of day visitors come to enjoy on bank holiday weekends. The Burford Bridge Hotel at the foot of the hill was where Horatio Nelson spent his last night with Emma Hamilton in 1805, before sailing off to embrace victory and death at the Battle of Trafalgar. John Keats (1795–1821) stayed here, too, in the winter of 1819, and climbed Box Hill by moonlight, as recalled in his long poem *Endymion*:

> O thou wouldst joy to live in such a place! ...
> For by one step the blue sky shouldst thou find,
> And by another, in deep dell below,
> See, through the trees, a little river go ...

In nearby Shere (called 'the prettiest village in Surrey', and certainly calendar-neat and comely) the Norman Church of St James contains wonderful medieval stained glass and memorial brasses, as well as

RIGHT: Leith Hill tower, founded on the tomb of its eccentric builder. From the top there is a stunning view over the North Downs.

BELOW: The ironworks and forges may have fallen silent, but the old hammer ponds in the Surrey woodlands have found a new lease of life as springtime havens for thousands of breeding frogs.

ABOVE: The Norman church in Shere village, dedicated to St James, is a treasure chest of wonderful medieval art and craftsmanship, from the 14th-century stained glass to the ancient oak doors and the Mass sundials scratched into the stone doorways.

a tiny cell where anchoress Christine Carpenter was enclosed in 1329 to embark on a life of prayer in solitude. She apparently got out and 'ran about, being torn to pieces by attacks of the Tempter'. The church also holds a treasure as evocative as it is tiny: a miniature bronze icon of the Virgin and Child, only 2 inches (5 centimetres) tall, which was found by a dog in a bramble bush. The likelihood is that this little statuette was lost by some medieval pilgrim on the way to Canterbury along the ancient Pilgrim's Way.

The flinty sunken track known nowadays as the North Downs Way follows the course of the Pilgrim's Way for much of its length. A Pilgrim's Way it truly was in the Middle Ages, ridden or trodden by a dozen generations of English men and women as an act of piety and self-mortification. They followed its 100-mile (161-kilometre) course from Winchester, historic seat of kings, to England's prime medieval pilgrimage objective, the tomb of St Thomas à Becket at Canterbury. The *Canterbury Tales* travellers brought to life by Geoffrey Chaucer (c.1345–1400) with their earthy anecdotes and morality, rode this same Pilgrim's Way. But the ancient trackway has almost certainly been in use since Stone Age times, a route across southern England that enabled travellers to stay high above the bogs, forests and unknown dangers of the valley floors. You can see for miles from the Pilgrim's Way, walking among the trees and across the open downland shoulders on a track printed broad and deep by the feet, hooves and wooden wheels of many millennia.

Both Chiltern Hills and North Downs are all too popular with Londoners. Far less frequented, and much less

compromised, are the heaths and commons that still grace the Home Counties between the inexorably spreading blotches of housing development. Ashtead and Epsom commons, smothered with pollarded and coppiced woodland, are typical; more sombre and moody are the wild miles of Chobham Common just outside the ring of the M25, one of southern Britain's largest stretches of undeveloped and unimproved lowland heath. Heather, bracken, gorse and broom flourish in the sandy soil; foxes and badgers, roe deer and voles thrive here, along with 30 kinds of butterfly and 10 times that number of spider species. Hobbies twist low over the heath, and nightjars hunt moths after dark by means of radar signals that they receive in the network of whiskers round their beaks.

The heaths are beautiful, though their attractions can only be properly appreciated by those who take plenty of time to explore. In the 18th century they were seen as 'a vast tract of land given up to barrenness,' according to the *Journal* of Daniel Defoe (1660–1731), 'horrid and frightful to look upon; not only good for little, but good for nothing.'

Defoe was echoing the opinion of his day and age, when the commons and heaths near London were seen as sinister badlands, useless for agriculture and infested with highwaymen and other vagabonds. But today's eyes focus differently. Those who trouble to put on some waterproof boots, leave at home their prejudices and take with them a pair of sharp eyes and a thirst for discovery, can walk out across the commons and savour the last true piece of wildness in all the cosseted Home Counties – a little pinch of pepper in the smooth soup of London's countryside.

ABOVE: Peaceful grazing in the glades of the well-wooded Chobham Common, one of the most unspoiled corners of the Home Counties.

# 2
# THE CHALK
# COUNTIES
## WHITE CLIFFS AND ROLLING DOWNS

ABOVE: The Tudor manor
house of Hever Castle,
where King Henry VIII
courted young Anne Boleyn.

OPPOSITE: The Seven Sisters
march eastwards towards
Beachy Head in Sussex –
Britain's most dramatic
stretch of chalk cliffs.

I T WAS COUNTLESS THOUSANDS of microscopically small sea creatures called *foraminifera* that formed the great blanket of chalk – up to 1,700 feet (518 metres) thick – that now covers a large swathe of southern England. The *foraminifera* lived and died in the Great Chalk Sea, a shallow tropical ocean that covered most of northern Europe a hundred million years ago. Their shells, piling up through the millennia, gradually compacted into the crumbly white rock. It billows and undulates, an elastic substructure under corn, grass and woods, for some 200 miles (322 kilometres) westward from Kent through Sussex, Hampshire and Wiltshire, down into nethermost Dorset, where it makes its final plunge into the English Channel around the Isle of Purbeck.

Greenstone and sandstone, tougher rocks, were pushed up through the chalk in some places by titanic subterranean movements. Across the Weald of Kent the white blanket bulged up into a dome shape, then weathered away to leave a rough tongue of sand and clay between the two eroded lips of chalk that we know today as the North and South Downs.

The Kentish Weald, a beautiful smother of oak, ash and beech woods, dips into secret hollows in the greensand. This is some of the most widespread broad-leaved woodland in Britain, clothing steep valleys that rise to ridgetop villages such as Ticehurst and red-tiled Goudhurst. Notable country houses sit like contented cats in this rich landscape: Penshurst Place, the magnificent 14th-century house where Elizabethan poet-soldier Sir Philip Sydney was born; Leeds Castle rising like a dream from its lake; Hever Castle, where Anne Boleyn grew up and caught the roving eye of King Henry VIII; the mellow Tudor brick and timber of Ightham Mote, girdled by a moat and haunted by a Grey Lady. Also characteristic of the Kentish countryside are the oasts with their conical white caps: they were used for drying hops, a very Kentish crop, until the advent of more modern brewing technology. The brewing of good beer is still a speciality of the county, though, with the Shepherd Neame brewery producing superb bitter brews in the traditional way.

Very different are the moody coastal landscapes that sandwich the Kentish Weald. Up north along the widening estuary of the sea-going River Thames are the broad, flat grazing marshes that Charles Dickens (1812–1870) knew in his boyhood, used by the Master so effectively in creating the menacing atmosphere in the opening chapters of *Great Expectations*. You can find the graveyard, at St Mary's Church near Higham, in which the runaway convict Magwitch leaped out on Pip and swung him upside down so that the church went head over heels. Cliffe Fort, a grim ruin on the Thames shore beyond, was where Pip ran through the fog on Christmas morning with a file and food for the convict. Egypt Bay, where the dreaded 'hulks' or derelict prison ships lay anchored, is a couple of miles downriver.

Down in the south-east tip of Kent, a line of ancient cliffs stands nearly 10 miles (15 kilometres) inland. Where they once dipped their feet in the English Channel is a great table-land of grazing marshes and arable fields, some 80 square miles (200 square kilometres) of ground clawed back from the sea by successive generations of reclaimers: Romans, monks, Dutchmen and locals. Romney Marsh, peppered with early medieval churches and shut-away villages, bearded with reeds and willows, thick with tales of smugglers, is a strange countryside. Even stranger is the shore landscape that bounds it on the south, the triangular neb of pebbles called Dungeness that forms the largest shingle beach in the world. The ugly grey cubes of a nuclear power station, monstrously out of scale, squat on the shingle. But somehow the spirit of the place reduces this eyesore to a pale ghost that fails to impinge. Here fishermen in tight-knit families – the Oillers, the Tarts – still go out after dab, mackerel and herring in clinker-built wooden boats with little mizzen sails. The shingle is dotted with their rough wood and concrete huts, and seamed with little railway lines down which the fishermen trundle their equipment on home-made flatbeds. Here some of the tarred black huts have been taken over by weekenders, but there are others occupied by fishermen, bait-sellers, eccentrics or bird-watchers – sometimes all these rolled into one. Dungeness is famous for bird-watching, as a prime landfall and haven for migrating species delighted to set foot on dry land after days over the sea. Whitethroats, flycatchers, warblers, terns, skua, scoter … the list lengthens.

ABOVE: Leeds Castle in Kent, often acclaimed as the most beautiful castle in Britain. The original Norman castle, built in stone around 1120, has been altered and added to over the years. Its history, too, has been a patchwork – King Edward I and Queen Eleanor built the keep in the 1280s, King Henry VIII made the castle a royal residence in Tudor times, and 100 years later it was used to house French prisoners of war.

Those who mean to get the most from their beach walks here take a pair of binoculars with them. On Dungeness, crunching into a stiff sea wind across the shingle, you can feel more exhilaratingly lonely than anywhere else in south-east England.

A walker clambering up to the higher country that rolls from those interior cliffs above Romney Marsh would meet the Pilgrim's Way at the eastern extremity of its run. Turning west along the old road, one could stride the ridge of the North Downs for 60 miles (100 kilometres) before crossing the county border into the woodlands of the Surrey Weald. That is the best possible way to savour the North Downs: on foot, with a week or two to spare for the journey. And the same goes for the other ridge that once formed the floor of the Great Chalk Sea: the South Downs. Running parallel with the North Downs and some 30 or 40 miles (50-65 kilometres) to the south, these South Downs are the pride of the county of Sussex, rolling shoulders of downland that billow up

OPPOSITE: Casting for a trout on the River Test in Hampshire. The clear waters of the downland rivers, running fast and shallow over gravel beds, are perfect for trout fishing. The Test is reckoned the finest in the world, hence the high charges for a prestigious fishing beat along its banks.

from the flatter lands around like a line of sails pegged loosely over an upward-roaring gale. 'The highest points command much of earth, all of heaven,' wrote Edward Thomas before the First World War. 'They are the haunt of the swift, the home of wheatear and lark and of whatsoever in the mind survives or is born in this pure kingdom of grass and sky.' When Thomas went striding across the Downs they were still largely covered in short herb-rich turf, used for sheep-grazing. Two world wars saw them ploughed up and seeded for corn production. Some of the old downland has

remote enough these days to escape the sullen grumble of a road in the distance. But Jefferies's comments on the timeless and seemingly motionless effect of walking on the Downs still hold good for the tired hiker: 'Like rowing at sea, you row and row and row, and seem where you started – waves in front and waves behind; so you may walk and walk and walk, and still there is the intrenchment on the summit, at the foot of which, well in sight, you were resting some hours ago.' And still, tucked down into one of the green declivities below the Iron Age fort of Cissbury Ring or under the beech and oak blankets of East Dean and West Dean Woods, you can still revel in silence and solitude.

The Sussex coast is thoroughly built up, in an almost continuous 30-mile (48-kilometre) strip from Brighton to Chichester. 'Old Ocean's Bauble, glittering Brighton' has never lost its raffish appeal as the south coast's premier seaside resort. The splendidly tacky delights of the Palace Pier, opened in 1899 and still a mecca for slot machine connoisseurs, are a 'do-not-miss' treat for any visitor to the town. The wide waters of Chichester Harbour, bellying out inside the tight belt of East Head and Hayling Island, provide a bracing contrast. Pretty waterside villages such as Bosham and West Itchenor face the shore with the long shallow swell of the South Downs as a distant backdrop – best seen on a sunny day from a sailing boat scudding through the green, wind-whipped water of the harbour.

ABOVE: The blacksmith's forge, once a familiar part of the village scene but now a rare survival, continues to turn out ironwork at the excellent Weald and Downland Open Air Museum at Singleton in West Sussex.

survived, or been painstakingly recreated, rich in small chalk grassland flowers and songbirds. The old rural crafts and ways of farming, too – charcoal-burning, corn-stooking, the building of hayricks and sheepfolds – are kept alive at the superb Weald & Downland Museum at Singleton in West Sussex.

The Downs are not as quiet as they were. In the 1870s Richard Jefferies (1848–1887) could write, 'There is no noise ... the long, long slopes, the endless ridges, the gaps between, hazy and indistinct, are absolutely without noise.' Thirty years later, that quintessential downland writer W. H. Hudson (1841–1922) noted in *Nature in Downland*: 'The quiet [of the Downs] becomes increasingly grateful, and the contrast between the hills and the lowland grows sharper with each day ... The coarse and common sounds of the lowlands do not penetrate into the silent country of the hills.' Nowadays an honest walker on the South Downs Way could not claim as much. On the top of the Sussex downs you are seldom

Soft and beautiful Hampshire is Sussex's westerly neighbour, a county of chalk streams famous for trout-fishing, of gentle downland clothed with beech hangers in the north and east, and down in the south-west the wide swathe of the New Forest. In some Hampshire woods the ancient craft of coppicing – harvesting the shoots of hazel and beech – is still carried on; the coppiced wood is used to make fencing and tool handles, or for firewood. The River Test is the best-known trout stream in England, with its clear shallow water running fast over gravel and trailing waterweed, its overhanging willows, its many parallel courses that join and separate a dozen times in a couple of miles. A sunny morning along the Test may be crowned with a fat trout on the fly, but it hardly matters if there is not a single bite. Above roll the Downs; it was on the northward-facing brow of these, just south of Newbury, that Richard Adams (b. 1920) dreamed up the Honeycomb burrow which became the home of Hazel, Fiver, Bigwig and the other famous rabbits of *Watership Down*. There really is a Watership Down in just the right spot, and a beech tree inscribed 'Big Wig'; and with persistence and a nose in the book you can follow the rabbits' epic trek to safety in the Honeycomb, and their subsequent journeys to Efrafa,

the grim barracks complex of a warren commanded by that ferocious megalomaniac buck, General Woundwort.

Across the tidal narrows of the Solent from Southampton lies the diamond-shaped Isle of Wight, a favourite holiday destination, yet a place with its own strong character and traditions. And the New Forest, beyond the urban sprawl of Southampton, is also a place apart. This is Britain's largest stretch of broad-leaved forest: a true forest in the original sense of a mosaic of trees, water, wetland, farmland and heath. The New Forest ponies – wild-roaming descendants of horses

ABOVE: Semi-wild ponies graze the open commons of the New Forest.

RIGHT: Jane Austen's house, in the village of Chawton near Winchester, is now a museum dedicated to the writer, and attracts Austen fans from all over the world.

BELOW: Photographed in the half light, a pair of badgers caught out in the open is a rare sight. These wary nocturnal creatures find safe haven in their deep-dug earth 'sets' or burrows in the depths of the New Forest.

that came ashore in 1588 from the shipwrecked galleons of the Spanish Armada, some say – are well known. Less frequently seen are the deer, foxes, badgers and frogs that share the depths of the Forest with wild flowers, lichens, mosses, butterflies and birds. The 'commoners' or residents exercise their jealously guarded rights to cut turf for fuel, gather firewood and graze pigs on beechmast and acorns. An ancient Court of Verderers upholds Forest Law, some of it picturesquely archaic, some still of practical conservation value. The Forest in its springtime haze of green, or its autumnal coat of many colours, is a famed beauty spot; it is also a carefully managed reserve for wildlife.

Two writers of widely differing type celebrated the pleasures of central Hampshire. Jane Austen (1775–1817) did so in the imagination, through her books written at

home in Steventon and Chawton; while just down the road at Selborne the country curate and naturalist Gilbert White (1720–1793) kept his diary stocked with meticulous detail of the most realistic kind. How White loved his house, 'The Wakes', his garden, and the steep escarpments, beech hangers and commons all round Selborne. His collection of letters, *The Natural History and Antiquities of Selborne*, was published in 1788, and has become during the intervening two centuries one of the best-selling books in the English language. His love for his native village and the deep, secretive countryside shines out from its pages, as do his astonishing powers of observation and deduction of all things natural: how fallow deer can breathe underwater by means of vents in the corners of their eyes; how vinegar will not dissolve the local freestone;

why thrushes dig out cuckoo-pint roots in snowy weather; the copulation of frogs, the orgasms of swifts and the eating of red mice by dogs. His account of air-borne spiders' webs was set down in a letter written in 1776, some 34 years after he had witnessed the sight.

'About nine an appearance very unusual began to demand our attention, a shower of cobwebs falling from very elevated regions, and continuing, without any interruption, till the close of day. These webs were not single filmy threads, floating in the air in all directions, but perfect flakes or rags; some near an inch broad, and 5 or 6 long, which fell with a degree of velocity which showed they were considerably heavier than the atmosphere.

'On every side as the observer turned his eyes might he behold a continued succession of fresh flakes falling

ABOVE: Selborne Common stretches away across the high ground above Gilbert White's old home, The Wakes, in the Hampshire village of Selborne. The common contains many ancient trees that the curate-naturalist would have known and studied more than 200 years ago.

into his sight, and twinkling like stars as they turned their sides towards the sun ...'

Gilbert White was also a lover of the Sussex Downs, and mused on their origins as much poetically as scientifically:

'For my own part, I think there is somewhat peculiarly sweet and amusing in the shapely figured aspect of chalk-hills ... I never contemplate those mountains without thinking I perceive somewhat analogous to growth in their gentle swellings and smooth finger-like protuberances, their fluted sides, and regular hollows and slopes, that carry at once the air of vegetative dilation and expansion ... Was there ever a time when these immense masses of calcareous matter were thrown into fermentation by some adventitious moisture; were raised and leavened into such shapes by some plastic power; and so made to swell and heave their broad backs into the sky so much above the less animated clay of the wild below?'

The idea of the Downs puffing upwards, like bread dough under the influence of some yeast-like catalyst, is a splendid one. Gilbert White reveals himself as one of the best kinds of natural scientists, open to wonder,

painstaking and precise, yet ready to make giant leaps of the imagination.

From Hampshire the chalk has more marching still to do, west and south through Wiltshire. Prehistoric mystery clings to this great ragged circle of a county in a network of ancient lines, sites and nodes. The 5,000-year-old Ridgeway, under its modern guise of a National Trail long-distance footpath, travels in a westward extension of the Icknield Way from Ivinghoe Beacon in

the Chiltern Hills as far as Overton Hill near Avebury, a famous archaeological site. Avebury is an astonishing place, a small village enclosed in a great earth bank studded with giant standing stones. Two smaller circles stand shoulder to shoulder inside the bigger one. Some of these stones are thickly cowled with legend: the Diamond Stone performs a stately pirouette at midnight, the Devil's Stone vomits forth smoke if anyone is daring enough to sit on it. Fact goes with fancy, too. Medieval dwellers in Avebury pushed many of the stones over to dispel their demonic powers, and on one of these wrecking sessions some time during the 14th century the village surgeon-barber was unlucky enough to be caught in the path of a toppling stone. They dug his skeleton out in 1938, crushed as flat as a board, with coins in his pouch and his barber's scissors lying beside him.

From Avebury, the Avenue, a mile-long (1.6-kilometre-long) way flanked by standing stones, leads to the

ABOVE: The white horse carved into the chalk turf of a Wiltshire hillside.

RIGHT: Ancient men raised Silbury Hill for some compelling but long-forgotten purpose. This 130-ft (40-m), flat-topped mound was the result of years of planning and hard work, founded as it is on a pyramidal internal structure of cut chalk blocks. In its original aspect, a dazzling white mini-mountain of chalk, it must have looked truly spectacular. Was it raised in honour of Suil the Eye Goddess, or Sil the Sun Goddess? No-one can say for sure.

RIGHT: The Angel Hotel, one of many beautifully preserved medieval buildings in the National Trust's village of Lacock, Wiltshire. The National Trust acquired Lacock in 1944 as a gift from the descendants of William Fox Talbot (1800–1877), inventor of the modern photographic negative, who lived at Lacock Abbey.

Sanctuary, two concentric rings of stones. Nearby rises Silbury Hill, a flat-topped mound 130 feet (40 metres) high above a core of chalk-block walls that radiate out from a central hub. What caused men to build this artificial hill 4,500 years ago, taking a decade and shifting over a million cubic feet (30,000 cubic metres) of chalk to do so? There is no doubt, at any rate, about the purpose of West Kennet Long Barrow just south of Avebury. Constructed some 600 or 700 years before Silbury Hill, this is the largest chambered tomb in England, and was used to hold the remains of the privileged dead for at least 1000 years.

Wiltshire's prime prehistoric monument, of course, is the mighty structure of Stonehenge, which dominates the downland 20 miles (32 kilometres) to the south. The great trilithons circle round like doorways into space, the centrepiece of a landscape pimpled with Stone Age and Bronze Age burial mounds. Through the site runs another ancient trackway, in fact Britain's oldest road – the Harroway, already 3,000 years old when the first earthworks of Stonehenge were begun around 2950 BC. In that era, the distribution of Cornish tin across southern Britain may have provided the impetus for pioneer bronze-makers to link up sections of local trackway into one long-distance route high above the dangers of the valley floors. But what motivated their Stone Age forerunners to beat out the first downland tracks is anyone's guess.

In the south-eastern corner of Wiltshire lies Salisbury, the county town, set among the wide meadows of the

ABOVE: Britain's most famous archaeological monument, the enigmatic Bronze Age structure of Stonehenge. The 80 mighty dolerite stones known as 'bluestones' that were set up in a double circle in about 2100 BC were brought to Wiltshire from the Preseli Hills in western Pembrokeshire some 150 miles (240 km) away – a feat of prehistoric transport organisation that almost beggars belief.

River Avon. The Normans tried to plant a cathedral city within Iron Age ramparts on a round hilltop north of the Avon, but lack of water had forced the inhabitants down into the river valley by 1220. Here they built their magnificent new cathedral in pale Chilmark stone. A century later a spire was added – and what a spire! At 404 feet (123 metres) it is the tallest in Britain, a slender silvery needle that pierces the sky over the little city as a landmark for many miles around. North of Salisbury stretches the vast open expanse of Salisbury Plain, almost 100,000 acres (40,470 hectares) that have been owned, trained over, fired at and driven across by the Army since before the First World War. The public has been largely excluded for all that time, with the result that wildlife thrives undisturbed in a unique landscape.

Herb-rich sward, bare scrapes where stone curlew nest, Romano-British villages, Dark Ages field systems, chalk downs ... Well over half of all unimproved chalk downland left in Europe since the advent of modern agriculture is here on Salisbury Plain – riddled with high explosive, perhaps, but butterflies, deer, hares and birds do not bother overmuch about that. Nowadays walkers are permitted on the Plain on certain days and along certain routes, well away from firing areas, and those that venture there discover a landscape wild, horizon-sweeping and sombrely beautiful.

The chalk makes its final westward run through Dorset, plunging into the sea around the craggy cliffs of the Isle of Purbeck. Dorset is another county that benefits from the elasticity of chalk, rounded by weather into downland and valleys that call a walker onward. This is

history-rich Wessex, where two centuries ago Mary Anning found a prehistoric fish lizard curving from the slippery cliffs of Black Ven. Here fossil ammonites strew the beaches around Lyme Regis, a priapic chalk-cut giant bestrides the hill above Cerne Abbas, and swans still flock at Abbotsbury's medieval swannery in the shelter of the mighty shingle bank of Chesil Beach.

Bare and beautiful, Dorset is above all the haunt of Thomas Hardy (1840–1928). The writer-poet's Higher Bockhampton birthplace is one of Dorset's prettiest cottage-and-garden ensembles. But it is out on the bleaker downs, across chalk and flint ploughlands the colour of milky coffee, and down in the rural towns and villages – Beaminster (Hardy's 'Emminster'), Sherborne ('Sherton Abbas'), Puddletown ('Weatherbury'),

Dorchester ('Casterbridge') – that Hardy-lovers feel closest to their idol as they identify scene after scene from his books, visit his house at Max Gate or sit to meditate in the village church where he sang and played his fiddle as a boy. There is eye-catching country all around hereabouts, but its beauty is often of a harsh kind, still closely linked to the practicalities of ploughing and sowing, milking and slaughtering that Hardy portrayed so realistically in his novels.

At Lyme Regis in the south-western corner of Dorset the chalk and greensand cliffs sit precariously on a greasy skid-mat of gault. Frequently they lurch seaward, cracking the ground and spewing falls of rock onto the beach. West of Lyme the coast forms a series of giant corrugations, now overrun with undisturbed woodland: a tangled jungle known as the Undercliff, home to dozens of bird, plant, insect and animal species. Novelist John Fowles (b. 1926), living and writing in Dorset a century after Thomas Hardy, immortalised the Undercliff in *The French Lieutenant's Woman*. Walking the single-track footpath through the 5 miles (8 kilometres) of greenery with only the waves and the birds to disturb the peace, you can feel truly alone, at times disturbingly so. This little paradise between the sky and the pebbly Dorset beaches holds the spirit of a jungle or a remote forest: strange, intense and self-sufficient, neither accepting nor rejecting the wanderer, getting on with the simple business of existing.

ABOVE: The 11th-century Corfe Castle in Dorset's Isle of Purbeck was the scene of a heroic defence by Lady Bankes and a few retainers during the English Civil War.

# 3
# THE WEST

## THE LAID-BACK CHARM
## OF THE RURAL WEST COUNTRY

S A GEOGRAPHICAL AREA the West Country is a nebulous concept. Yet what is and what is not included in that portmanteau term is as instinctively understood by the British as is the concept of East Anglia, the Welsh Borders or the Scottish Highlands. Greenly rolling countryside, rocky coves and surf-pounded beaches, dense woods and lush meadows, rich butter and cream, a relaxed holiday atmosphere, ruddy-cheeked people with a rural way of talking so rich you could eat it with a spoon – all these are in the West Country mix.

Devon is unquestionably one of the gateways to the West Country. Stealing westward out of the chalk country into south-east Devon, all is sweet and gentle: plough furrows in red earth, the cattle grazing across green fields, green oakwoods. Exeter rises, its pale pink sandstone cathedral set like a cut stone in a green clasp. West of the city, though, the land takes a harsher turn altogether. It rises and hardens, pushing dark brown and slate blue ridges against the sky like a succession of petrified waves. Many are crested with the jagged outlines of tors, outcrops of granite. This is Dartmoor, the West Country's dourest landscape and one of the most atmospheric.

'As you value your life or your reason, keep away from the moor,' was the daunting anonymous message received by Sir Henry Baskerville at the outset of *The Hound of the Baskervilles*, the greatest Sherlock Holmes thriller that Sir Arthur Conan Doyle (1859–1930) ever wrote. In setting his fable of terror, cruelty and the Dark Powers in the wastes of the moor, Conan Doyle articulated a general perception of Dartmoor as a grim and forbidding place. It certainly can be all of that, especially up near the dismal stone fortress of Dartmoor prison, or when a walker senses himself lost in one of the moor's famous mists among the sodden peat bogs of Cranmere, marooned at the heart of Dartmoor in an end-of-the-world silence. 'The thing to be done by anyone who gets into such a bog,' opined Sabine Baring-Gould (1834–1924) in *A Book of Dartmoor*, 'is to spread his arms out – this will prevent his sinking – and if he cannot struggle out, to wait, cooling his toes in bog water, till assistance comes.' Baring-Gould, squire and rector of Lew Trenchard under the western edge of the moor, published *A Book of Dartmoor* in 1900. He was author of dozens of books, poems, hymns and articles, and wrote most of them standing up. A formidable man, but also one sensitive to the glories of nature in unlikely places – as on Dartmoor in the depths of winter:

'When below are mud and mist, aloft on the moor the ground is hard with frost and the air crisp and clear. Down below we are oppressed with the fall of the leaf, affecting us, if inclined to asthma and bronchitis; and in the short, dull days of December and January our spirits wax dark amidst naked trees and when our ankles

ABOVE: The clapper bridge at
Postbridge on Dartmoor,
long thought to be a
prehistoric structure, was
probably built in the 14th
century to carry the old
moorland track from Tavistock
to Moretonhampstead across
the East Dart River. When the
road was turnpiked in later
years, a new bridge (seen
in the background of this
photograph) superseded
the medieval clapper.

are deep in mud. There are no trees on Dartmoor to
expose their naked limbs, and tell us that vegetation is
dead. The shoulders of down are draped in brown seal-
skin mantles – the ling and heather, as lovely in its
sleep as in its waking state; the mosses, touched by
frost, turn to rainbow hues. For colour effects give me
Dartmoor in winter.'

Dartmoor can be beautiful in summer, too, especially
on one of those shining West Country days after a
period of rain when the air is glass clear and the wet
moor smells as rich as molasses. That is the time to go
exploring up the shallow, fast-flowing rivers: the East
Dart, for example, which comes down a bed of granite
boulders from the Cranmere heights to rush under the
medieval clapper bridge at Postbridge in the middle of
the moor. Scattered across the moor around Postbridge
are the remains of prehistoric dwellings. Up the East
Dart you can find tiny circular beehive huts, built of
stone by Iron Age farmers for themselves and their
families, and enigmatic stone circles like the Grey
Wethers standing out on the moor slopes far from any
motor road. On the ridge of Broad Down, overlooking
the river and the surrounding country, is Broadun
Ring, a great stone wall built 4,000 years ago to protect
a community of little round hut dwellings. Up here the

mind buzzes like a doorbell, a summons to open the
imagination wide and explore within.

Softer lands intervene as you travel on west from
Dartmoor, still cut with deep valleys such as Lydford
Gorge. A trail runs through the damp ferny depths of
the gorge where the notorious red-headed Gubbins
tribe would ambush, rob and murder travellers in the
wild and lawless days of 17th-century Dartmoor.

On Dartmoor's sister wilderness, across the River
Tamar in Cornwall, there were dark deeds, too, back in
the bad old days. Bodmin Moor is only half the size of
Dartmoor, but contains at its heart the same sense of
remoteness and of bleak beauty. Only a few miles from
the coves and caves of the north Cornwall coast, the
moor and its lonely inns were ideal hangouts for smugglers – not least among them Jamaica Inn, smack dab
in the middle of the moor. When Daphne du Maurier
(1907–1989) stumbled into the bar out of a moor mist
in 1930, her febrile imagination responded to the tall
tales she heard by weaving a classic smuggling yarn
around the old pub. These days holidaymakers' cars
run nose to tail along the A30 dual carriageway that
slices past the spot, and the romance of Jamaica Inn
draws hordes in to see where Mary and her dastardly
uncle battled to outwit each other. But you can walk

out of earshot of all that in five minutes: south on a path to Dozmary Pool where (some say) Sir Bedivere flung the mighty sword Excalibur on the orders of the dying King Arthur, or north towards Brown Willy and Rough Tor, summits of the moor. Not far off to the east are other famous Bodmin Moor sites, both manmade and natural: the triple stone circles of the Hurlers (local ball players turned into stone for impiously playing on the Sabbath), Trethevy Quoit's stone burial chamber, and the great piled tor of the Cheesewring, as high as a house, tottering on slender legs of granite undercut by wind and weather over millennia.

Every true Cornishman knows that foreigners begin east of the Tamar. Cornwall was always a hard place for hard-won livings, underground in the tin mines, up top on small windblown farms, or out in wild Atlantic or treacherous Channel seas on a fishing boat. When times got too tough back in the 18th and 19th

LEFT: The capstone of Trethevy Quoit burial chamber, held aloft on sturdy flanking stones, weighs several tons.

BELOW: The outcrops of Combestone Tor, near the eastern edge of Dartmoor, have weathered into fantastic shapes as the frost and rain of millennia have gradually widened cracks and crevices in the granite.

ABOVE: The picturesque south
Cornwall harbour of
Mevagissey.

centuries. 'Cousin Jack' emigrated by the hundred thousand to seek mining or fishing employment all over the world. Then the Romantic movement introduced to fine society the notion that a savage granite coast and weatherbeaten fishing villages huddled in the cliffs could be attractive, sources of aesthetic pleasure rather than primitive dread. The railways came in the 19th century and ushered in holidaymakers by the million. Cornish beaches, sandy enough for the tiniest toddler yet pounded with enough wild rollers to satisfy the freakiest surfboarder, figure in *Summoned by Bells*, the wonderfully nostalgic blank verse autobiography of Sir John Betjeman (1906–1984). This poem is the crystallisation of most middle-aged

British holidaymakers' childhood memories of 'safe Cornish holidays before the storm'.

Cornwall is a narrowing leg of land, bent south-westwards from the thick knee of the Devon/Cornwall border country. The south coast is sheltered along its Channel shores; the north is open to the full force of the Atlantic. Cornwall's southern coast is seeded with fishing villages whose whitewashed houses under slate or thatch are piled prettily above their small, heavily built harbours. Looe, Polperro, Mevagissey, Portloe, Porthleven: the old pilchard-storage sheds and the fishermen's cottages (built three storeys high so that fishing gear could be stored in the ground floor), done up for holiday homes or lived in by incomers from 'across the Tamar', are as picturesque as any camera-snapper could wish for. Tucked away up the river creeks that penetrate far inland are bigger towns such as Fowey and Falmouth, with their ferries buzzing to and fro across the rivers and the occasional big freighter lumbering upriver to anchorage. Away from these tourist-orientated honey traps are grittier sides to Cornwall: near St Austell the mini-mountains of blinding white china clay spoil known as the Cornish Alps, or the windy open spaces of the uncrowded Lizard Peninsula out towards the western tip of Cornwall. At Lizard Town, the southernmost point of the British mainland, the splendid lighthouse has recently been automated; visitors can admire its hundreds of rainbow polished curves of lantern glass, and the antique

ABOVE: In spite of modern fishing technology, Cornish fishermen still have to mend and sort their nets by hand.

LEFT: Commercialism cannot sully the myth-haunted, rugged landscape of Land's End.

motors tended by generations of lighthouse keepers.
Another Lizard tradition is jealously maintained, too –
the manufacture of the best Cornish pasties in the
world. The little shop that sells them, set back from the
lane to Landewednack, can hardly keep pace with
demand in the holiday season.

Out at the very end of Cornwall, past the money-
spinning synthetic 'Land's End Experience', lies the
real Land's End itself, a craggy nest of granite pinnacles. They dip to water that can lie as smooth as silk,
can raise a lazy, treacherous swell to suck you off a
rock, or can thump against the land with the hammer
blows of a furious giant. This is proper, elemental
Cornwall, a place where fishermen drown and farmers

ABOVE: The thatched Rising Sun Hotel, parts of which date back 700 years, stands at the foot of Mars Hill in Lynmouth on the north Devon coast. Local stories say that smugglers once hid their contraband in the inn.

RIGHT: Wild Exmoor ponies. The pony herds – augmented by animals bred up and introduced by the Exmoor National Park authorities – are descended from hill stock that has been native to the moor for thousands of years.

curse their luck, where massive stone tombs and granite circles on the moors hint at the preoccupations of people struggling to stay alive in a harsh place thousands of years ago.

Fantasy rides high here, not least with the Scilly Isles whose pinprick shapes on the sea horizon can be made out from Land's End on the clearest of days, nearly 30 miles (48 kilometres) away down in the south-west. Did the five Scilly islands, glimpsed on the skyline by Old Age romantics, metamorphose into the famed and fabulous Atlantis, the golden sea city overwhelmed by the waves? Certainly such a place, the land of Lyonesse, exists in West Country mythology. Some tales hold that the last battle between King Arthur and his black-hearted kins-man Mordred took place there; other versions have it that the brave knight Tristan was conceived in Lyonesse and born in a boat bringing his mother to the mainland.

One story tells how a Lyonesse hero, one Tresilian, was the only survivor of a cataclysm that burst in the walls of the fair land, galloping hell-for-leather across the sand for the safety of mainland Cornwall with a gigantic wave sucking at his horse's heels. And some say they can hear the golden bells of Lyonesse tolling beneath the sea on stormy nights ...

The north coast of Cornwall has its holiday towns: St Ives, so favoured by artists, on a striking curve of sand; loudly disco-fevered Perranporth with its straight 3-mile (5-kilometre) run of sandy beach; jolly, bustling Newquay. There are much harsher scenes, too, of Cornwall's ancient and now defunct tinning industry. Ruined engine-houses, tall and blank-eyed, raise their admonitory fingers of chimneys heavenwards around the former mining villages of St Agnes, Camborne and Redruth. Mining heaps and holes, shafts and buildings dot the landscape. But the coast is magnificent, all steep cliffs and little bays, its great inlet of the Camel Estuary scattered with the triangular sails of sailing boats like a sprinkling of minute white sharks' teeth.

A lusty and lovely mermaid, shaped with artless gusto by some forgotten woodcarver 600 years ago, enlivens an ancient bench-end in St Senara's Church at Zennor. In local legend it was she who enticed young Matthew Trewhella into her sea-girt cave in order to have his silver-voiced singing all to herself. Another legend places another golden city in Cornwall, this time under the high dunes of Penhale Sands behind Perranporth Beach. It was the lechery of the high-born women of Langarrow that caused their city to be buried under the sands, when they tired of their blanched and flabby husbands and began to take lovers among the

ABOVE: Watersmeet, a famous Exmoor beauty spot near Lynton. Hereabouts Henry Williamson set one of the most exciting scenes in *Tarka the Otter*, where the hunted Tarka escapes from the jaws of his implacable enemy Deadlock the hound, and almost drowns him for good measure.

ABOVE: Legends of King Arthur and of the youthful Jesus gather thickly around Somerset's hippy mecca, Glastonbury Tor.

lowly criminals who made Langarrow rich by their sweated labour in the tin mines. Langarrow declined to a sink of iniquity, an offence to gods and men until it was blotted out for ever in a three-day sandstorm.

Strange stories, and stranger still are the Padstow Obby Osses, two demonic caped beasts with birdlike faces that caper through the streets of the little harbour town on May Day. Padstow heaves at the seams on that day, tens of thousands of onlookers delighting in the prancing Osses and their High-Stepping Teasers as the verses of the May Song are sung vigorously by dancers and spectators:

The young men of Padstow might if they would,
They might have built a ship and gilded her with gold ...
The young women of Padstow might if they would,
They might have made a garland with the white rose and the red ...

The Oss sinks down, submissive in death, as the dancers mourn him gently in a minor key:

Up flies the kite and down falls the lark O;
Aunt Ursula Birdhood she had an old ewe,
And she died in her own park O.

Then up jumps the Oss, reborn; up leap the dancers, and they jig on as everyone roars out the refrain to the stomach-gripping thump of bass drums:

Unite and unite and let us all unite,
For summer is acome unto day;
And whither we are going we will all unite
In the merry morning of May!

Across the Tamar and into north Devon, the third of the West Country's three great moors sprawls across the Devon–Somerset border. Exmoor is almost the complete antithesis of Dartmoor. This expanse of upland country is certainly lonely in parts: up till a couple of hundred years ago there were no roads over the moor, and the inhabitants were a pretty rugged bunch. R. D. Blackmore (1825–1900) immortalised the murderous Doone family in his 1869 classic *Lorna Doone*, basing the yarn on a real clan of robbers who holed up in a hidden valley deep in the moor, from which they would mount raids on remote farmsteads. But little of doom and gloom hangs about Exmoor as it does over the sombre wastes of Dartmoor. Sandstone underlies Exmoor, lending it a warmth and light denied to its granite-founded sister moor. Much of the moor is cattle-grazing, striped with stone walls or hedges: not exactly a tame environment, but one in accommodation rather than contention with man.

England's largest herd of red deer inhabits Exmoor, its freedom to roam uninhibitedly and to gobble crops tolerated by the moor farmers who like to hunt the deer. These are beautiful beasts, wary of humans and apt to be glimpsed cantering away over the skyline or disappearing into one of the thickly wooded combes or moor valleys. Since conservation measures have begun to take hold on the moor there has been a cautious return by otters, wiped out in the 1950s by pollution and inimical farming methods. Such news delights lovers of the writing of Henry Williamson (1895–1977). Williamson, a disillusioned and difficult man profoundly damaged by his experiences in the trenches of the First World War, settled in north Devon on the western fringe of Exmoor in 1921 and embarked as a complete unknown on the life of a writer. Seven years later his name and fame were made by his masterpiece, *Tarka the Otter* – often seen these days as a children's story, but in fact one of the most meticulously observed and sensitively handled works of nature writing ever produced. Most of *Tarka* is set on

ABOVE: 'Hatfuls, capfuls, Three bushel bags full, And a little heap under the stairs'. – An old Somerset apple-tree wassailing song.

LEFT: The old-fashioned rural practice of shoeing a horse still relies on individual skill.

Exmoor: the hunts, chases, matings, explorations and hair's-breadth escapes immerse readers in the very bones and lifeblood of the moor. Armchair travel at Williamson's elbow is wonderful; but being out there is better still, from the high heathery expanses at the crown of the moor to the cliffs that bend like rounded green knees into the muddy waters of the Bristol Channel – the Severn Sea, as old-fashioned Westcountrymen still like to call it.

The mighty River Severn brushes the flank of Somerset all the way up, narrowing from a broad arm of the sea to a probing finger poking far up into the body of the land. The turbulent Severn Estuary with its violent tides and strong salt and mud smells makes a curious companion for a county so rooted inland. Somerset's image is of bucolic slowness, of milking herds on broad green meadows and of rustic farmers

LEFT: Haymaking at Horton, Somerset, the old-fashioned way – by timeless skill of hand, and the use of tools unchanged since grandfather's day.

with the scrumpy jar permanently upended at their lips. There's some truth in it. But Somerset is a county of tremendous variety, too. The wide, flat Levels, a 500-square-mile (1,295-square-kilometre) saucer of peatland set between the Quantock and Mendip hills, have an atmosphere more East Anglian than West Country. The Quantocks are close to Exmoor, in characteristics as well as in geography; they echo the high sweep of the moor, the combes full of oak and ash woods, the red deer and the rounded sea coast. Mendip, by contrast, straddles the waist of the county as a limestone barrier, its flanks geometrically walled into productive fields at the time of the 18th- and 19th-century Enclosures, its bald heights scrubby with thin grass over outcropping limestone. The heart of Mendip is riddled with caves, a subterranean honeycomb of passages and openings reamed out by water over millions of years. Here, cavers wriggle through constricted squeezes and inch their way down slippery calcite formations, stalactites and fairy-like rock bridges in caverns as big as cathedrals, undreamed of by those who stay 'up top'. Some of the Mendip caves have been opened to the public for underground tours. The best-known of these show caves are in the flanks of the dramatic gorge above the village of Cheddar. Cheddar is famous for something else, too – the tasty, tangy cheese that used to be made in its namesake village. These days, while you can buy Canadian, Irish and Scottish 'Cheddar' in the supermarkets, the best Cheddar cheese is still made in Somerset and slowly matured to give it that unique nutty savour. What better accompaniment to a nice piece of Cheddar than a glass of that peculiarly potent and cloudy cider known as 'scrumpy'? There are plenty of farms making and selling this nectar in Somerset, especially on the Levels. Be warned, though: a little scrumpy goes a long way with the uninitiated, particularly on a hot day.

Two beautiful small cities crown this more northerly part of Somerset. Under Mendip sits Wells, a charming little place that is England's smallest city, presided over by the ship-like bulk of its great Gothic cathedral. The west front of Wells Cathedral, an early English masterpiece set with 300 outsize statues of saints, prelates and kings, is reckoned the finest in Europe; it is a jaw-dropping sight, especially on first viewing as you approach across the close and see the scale and elaboration of the design.

Up across Mendip, on the northern border of Somerset, the glorious Georgian ensemble of Bath

LEFT: Cheddar Gorge, the remnant of a mighty water-burrowed cave in the limestone flank of the Mendip Hills.

ABOVE: The agriculture
of Somerset is usually
associated with dairying and
cider orchards. But there is
also a good productive corn
belt around the waist of the
county, as witness these fine
cornfields near the ancient
Wessex capital of Somerton.

is one of the most visited tourist attractions in Britain. No wonder, with so many beautiful showpiece buildings filling the little town in its hollow of hills. The Romans did not discover the healing springs at Bath; they only embellished what the locals had been using since time out of mind. But it was in Queen Anne's time that Bath became the acme of fashion, when Beau Nash as Master of Ceremonies ruled the town and its balls and receptions with a rod of iron, dictating the exact requirements of dress, manners and custom by which water-drinkers and spa-loungers had to abide

if they wished to be accepted. Thousands of well-to-do folk did, and paid for superbly beautiful houses and public buildings to be designed by the father-and-son team of John Wood, Elder and Younger. With the harmonious sweep of the Royal Crescent, the beautifully restored Theatre Royal, the Pump Room and Assembly Rooms all carefully restored, you can stroll around Bath and fancy yourself arm in arm with Miss Jane Austen or the Prince Regent.

Where Bath is all carefully balanced art and artifice, neighbouring Bristol has a rough-and-ready air.

But you shouldn't leave the West Country without tipping your hat to this hilly old port with its city centre quays and waterways. Bristol has character, partly owed to the visionary genius of its benefactor, the great 19th-century engineer Isambard Kingdom Brunel. He was not a native of Bristol, but Brunel knew a good place for business when he found one. Through the city runs his monumental Great Western Railway, its cathedral-like station of Temple Meads exuding consequence. Here is the Floating Harbour he designed, and the pioneering steamship *Great Britain* he built. And spanning the muddy tidal waters of the Avon Gorge leaps Brunel's iconic Clifton Suspension Bridge, an airy double bow both strong and breathtakingly beautiful that perfectly catches the enterprising spirit of his age.

BELOW: Epitome of Victorian engineering genius: Isambard Kingdom Brunel's strong yet graceful Clifton Suspension Bridge spans the Avon Gorge at Bristol.

# 4
# WALES

## FROM THE VALLEYS TO THE MOUNTAINS

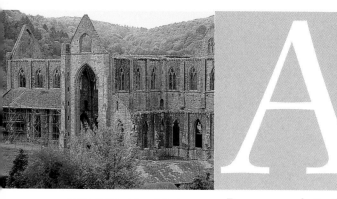

ABOVE: Stonework as delicate
as lace: the beautiful ruins of
the Cistercian abbey at
Tintern in the Wye Valley, on
the border between Wales
and England. Tintern Abbey
was founded in 1131, but
what remains of the buildings
today dates mostly from the
13th and 14th centuries.

OPPOSITE: The hilly
landscape so characteristic
of mid-Wales.

A COASTING SHIP MAKING INLAND up the estuary of the River Severn has the English counties of North Devon and Somerset for travelling companions on its right hand. On its left, all the way for 100 miles (160 kilometres), strides the southern coast of Wales. At the mouth of the Bristol Channel, 50 miles (80 kilometres) of open sea separates the English and Welsh shores. But by the time the vessel has turned north-east and run up to pass under the twin Severn bridges near Bristol, a bare couple of miles divides the two countries.

For many people South Wales means the Valleys, those once-industrial clefts that snake north like shakily drawn fingers from a palm of coastal land around Newport and Cardiff. Ebbw Vale, Cwm Rhondda, Merthyr Tydfil, Tredegar, Abertillery: a roll call of heavy industry, of rich choral singing, of chapel and pub, muddy-kneed rugby teams and black-faced colliers. A smoky pall, grey rainy streets, with high, bleak hills looking down between the slagheaps. A hard land, and hard lives: hard work, hard play.

Two hundred years ago, almost all of the Valleys were quiet green sheep country. Then the burgeoning Industrial Revolution snapped its impatient fingers and commandeered the iron ore and coal lying beneath the hill slopes and valley floors. The long, narrow villages so characteristic of industrial South Wales began to squeeze up the Valleys in company with roads, canals and railways. By 1843, in Ebbw Vale alone, there were 24 coal mines, along with iron, copper and tin works. It was boom time. It was also the time of gigantic towering slagheaps, black and slimy rivers, noise and light both day and night, and elderly miners coughing up diseased lungs.

Scenes like that will never again be part of the Valleys landscape. Coal is no longer king; the Tower Colliery at Hirwaun is the only deep coal mine still working in the Valleys. The slagheaps are greening over, or being planted with forests, to turn them into little hills. The ironworks and pithead buildings are torn down, their reservoirs turned into fishing lakes, their tramways into footpaths and cycle routes. Walkers who would never have dreamed of exploring the Valleys in their industrial days are beginning to roam there, discovering the by-paths, the side cwms and the old sheep roads across the intervening hills. As for the people of the tight-knit Valleys communities, shaped and defined over two centuries by their work – they are adapting to the new life of light industry and leisure activities, or leaving the whole thing behind them in a new twist to the emigration story.

The coast of South Wales, like all the best apples, contains a couple of dark spots in its rind – the rapidly gentrifying docklands of Cardiff, the industrial pollutant sprawl of Port Talbot (no swimming in *those* waters if you don't wish your skin to glow in the dark), and the refineries and oil terminals of Milford Haven. But the rest

ABOVE: Southerndown, one of
the gems of the Glamorgan
Heritage Coast. This 14-mile
(23-km) stretch of the South
Wales coast west of Cardiff is
carefully protected from any
development. Instead of
coastal motor roads there are
footpaths, from which visitors
can enjoy an abundance of
wild flowers, birds and
animals in a wonderfully
peaceful environment.

is gorgeous. It starts with the Glamorgan Heritage
Coast that runs round the southernmost bulge of the
coastline for 14 miles (23 kilometres) west to the
Ogmore River: a stretch of coast in which there is no
seaside development, no industrial exploitation, no
commercialisation. The motor roads do not reach the
sea. Instead, you go on foot along the coast path
among banks of orchids and trefoils, watching pere-
grine falcons streak after pigeons, slipping between
rock pools and dipping in and out of caves. In one of
these, Reynard's Cave near Llantwit Major, the smug-
gler-pirate Colyn Dolphin met a nasty end by drowning. He was well and truly trapped, having been
buried up to his neck in the cave floor by rivals who
left him there to taste the next high tide. Local maid-
ens found a gentler use for the cave; they would try to
throw a pebble over the natural rock arch that hangs
just below the cave roof, and thus ensure their wedding day before the year was out.

Smugglers reappear again at Southerndown, where
across the headland called Trwyn y Witch, the Witch's
Nose, sprawl the foundation outlines and terrace walls
of Dunraven Castle. The castle itself was demolished in
1963, though the walled gardens remain as refurbished visitor attractions. But the weight of legends
around Dunraven Castle still hangs heavy.

The best tall tale concerns Walter Vaughan, Lord of
Dunraven, who takes to evil ways and to luring ships
to their doom by showing false lights from the deadly
cliff of the Witch's Nose. The blue-blooded wrecker is
in league with a local smuggler, Mat of the Iron Hand.
Unknown to Walter, however, the smuggler is nursing
hatred for his well-born colleague. Mat's iron hand is
a hook, worn in place of the hand that was cut off
long ago when his band of smugglers found themselves waylaid by the forces of law and order. It was
Walter Vaughan himself, in his then capacity as a
law-abiding magistrate, who ordered the fatal

LEFT: Rhossili Beach and Down on the Gower Peninsula, south Wales. The Coast Path, a designated National Trail, runs for 189 spectacularly beautiful miles (304 km) from Amroth, near Tenby, all around the south-western rim of Wales to finish at St Dogmaels near Cardigan.

BELOW: The stark remains of the 19th-century wreck *Helvetia* on Rhossili Beach; in the background is the tidal promontory of Worm's Head.

ambush, and Mat of the Iron Hand has neither forgotten nor forgiven.

Vengeance ripens when Walter lures a ship to its doom on Trwyn y Witch. A sole survivor struggles ashore. Mat of the Iron Hand, hiding on the rocks below, recognises him as Walter's long-lost son, exiled by his harsh-tempered father years before. Mat loses no time in slitting the young heir's throat. Then he slices off the corpse's hand with its tell-tale signet ring, and has the fiendish pleasure of laying it before the man for whom he has nursed such hatred down the years.

West beyond Port Talbot and Swansea bulges the bulbous peninsula of Gower. The Gower is a place apart, with its own mild micro-climate and richly varied vegetation. Lovers of shore creatures find rarities here. Oxwich, 'a beautiful movement in the symphony of Gower', is a tiny seaside village above a broad beach, with a fine ruined castle on the hill and a range of

ABOVE: A walker on the
Pembrokeshire Coast Path
ponders offshore rock stacks.

grassy dunes behind the sands that are maintained as a National Nature Reserve. Birds as rare as bitterns, purple herons, firecrest and marsh harrier have been seen here. There are well over 600 species of flowering plants and two dozen types of butterfly. Further along the Gower coast is the spectacular promontory of Worm's Head, named by Norsemen *Wurm*, meaning 'dragon'. Twice daily the sea cuts Worm's Head off from the mainland, and then the green double hump in the sea does indeed look like a westward-swimming monster. The expedition at low tide out to the dragon's nose, the cliffs of Outer Head, is one of the most exciting coastal scrambles in Britain. Once there, you are deafened by the shrieking of thousands of kittiwakes and gulls, and more than likely to be soaked with blow-hole spray if there is a heavy sea running. It's a wild, wave-worn place, a real fresh sea gasp.

West again sweeps the Pembrokeshire coast, fringed with small islands, cut with cliffs and sandy coves, a carefully warded national park in its own right. There are formidable sand dunes and beautiful winding estuaries around Laugharne, where Dylan Thomas

(1914–1953) spent the last few years of his short life in the Boat House on the shore:

... a seashaken house
On a breakneck of rocks
Tangled with chirrup and fruit ...

The coast gets wilder as it dips beyond the Victorian seaside resort of Tenby, down to the tall cliffs of pale limestone around St Govan's Head. There is a remarkable structure here, the tiny 13th-century Chapel of St Govan built into a crack in the cliff. Crippled pilgrims came here to bathe in the holy well below the chapel, and to squeeze into the narrow chamber just above the altar where they could venerate the corrugations in the rock walls – moulded there by the ribs of the hermit saint during his many lengthy prayer vigils, believers were told.

St Bride's Bay, out at the western extremity of Wales, is half enclosed by two great peninsular pincers. On the more northerly of these lies St David's, Britain's smallest city, with its great Norman cathedral squatting low. The coast around here is magnificent, a storm-carved succession of promontories, headlands and cliff-held bays. Iron Age field boundaries, Bronze Age tumuli and

LEFT: The Boat House at Laugharne, last home of Welsh national poet Dylan Thomas, who described it as ' ... a seashaken house On a breakneck of rock Tangled with chirrup and fruit.' Thomas would write in the garage shed just down the lane from the Boat House, looking out over the Taff Estuary. The poet lies buried in nearby Laugharne churchyard.

BELOW: St David's Cathedral (begun in 1180 and finished piecemeal over the following 350 years), at the western-most tip of Pembrokeshire.

Stone Age burial chambers and standing stones abound. The coast walking is as magnificent as the views, and tends to inspire a healthy appetite. Traditional Welsh cuisine is making a comeback after years of being dismissed as peasant fare. Particular delicacies include seafood such as sewin, a delicious fish, and cockles from Penclawdd; also Welsh black beef and mountain lamb (sweeter than valley-bred lamb, according to connoisseurs), and edible seaweeds which form the basis of the recipe for laver bread, a delectable treat.

Off the Pembrokeshire coast rides a scattered fleet of islands. Caldey Island, near Tenby, is thickly wooded and beautifully looked after, a slip of sea-encircled land lovingly maintained by the tiny community of Cistercian monks who live in the island monastery. Skokholm and Skomer islands, sentinels guarding Broad Sound on the southern side of St Bride's Bay, are nature reserves, low-lying islets abandoned by farmers and now managed for the benefit of the hundreds of thousands of seabirds that inhabit them. Skokholm, the more southerly of the two, preserves the farmhouse restored by Ronald Lockley when he and his wife Doris lived here between the wars. Lockley's *Dream Island*, his account of their lives on Skokholm, became a classic. Visitors can follow in his footsteps, staying in the farmhouse and helping with the work of planting, wall-building, scrub-clearing and recording the birds. Nearly 60,000 pairs of Manx shearwaters breed on Skokholm, riddling the turf covering of the little island with their burrows, and more than twice

are Wales's finest shellfish speciality. Cocklers go out at dawn to dig up the precious bivalve molluscs from their burrows in the sands of Penclawdd Bay, Dyfed.

that number breed on sister island Skomer across the sound – the largest breeding colony in the world. To sit out at night and hear their unearthly gabbling and the clatter of wings as they return to the nest is a spine-tingling, unforgettable experience.

Ramsey Island, off the cliffs just south of St David's Head, is twice the size of Skokholm; 700 acres (290 hectares) of island with two hilly peaks, a bird sanctuary separated from the mainland by Ramsey Sound. This is one of the most ferocious tide rips in Britain's waters. It is a sobering, awe-inspiring sight to stand on the cliffs watching the highway of white water sweep and twist by, whorling and agitating, while a noise halfway between a roar and a groan rises out of the channel.

The great lumpy circle of hilly back country that makes up the centre of Wales has always been thought of as poor land.

Alas, alas, poor Radnorshire!
Never a park, and never a deer;
Never a squire of five hundred a year -
Save Richard Fowler of Abbeycwmhir.

The old county of Radnorshire, at the heart of rural Wales, is still poor in economic terms, though fantastically rich in natural beauty. A walk across the waist of Wales on one of the ancient drove roads that criss-cross the country will show you villages and farms, churches and once-great houses, all tucked away in the folds of valleys or along the spines of hill ranges. Rivers with walkable footpaths include the Teifi, flowing down to Cardigan Bay, where round coracle boats can still be seen fishing; the Tywi, rushing noisily down from Llyn Brianne in the back hills of the Tywi Forest; the Trannon, gently running along its east–west valley in the lee of the Cambrian Mountains among hill slopes patched with small hedged fields like a quilt sewn of countless shades of green.

The sabre shape of Cardigan Bay forms the western edge of central Wales, a 100-mile (160-kilometre) curve. Estuaries cut in: the Dyfi, running up from Aberdovey; the sandy Mawddach pushing north-east from Barmouth; the Dwyryd in the crook of Tremadog Bay. Great mountains rise not far inland, principally Plynlimon behind Aberystwyth, and Cader Idris over

LEFT: Creigiau Eglwyseg
('Church Rocks') near
Llangollen make exciting
abseiling territory.

• 6 1

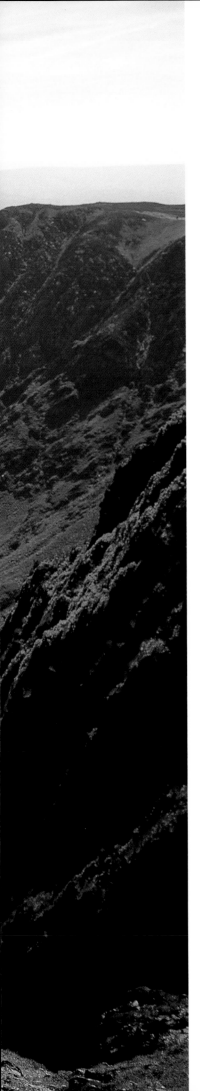

Barmouth. These are famous walking mountains, Cader Idris for its view (and for the old legend that he who climbs to the summit and sleeps there will awaken either a poet or a madman), and Plynlimon for its mists, bogs and multiple springs. Three great rivers have their source within a couple of miles of each other on the broad back of Plynlimon – Rheidol, Severn and Wye. George Borrow (1803–1881), the cross-grained East Anglian egotist and would-be Celt, made an ascent of the mountain in 1854 while researching for his master-piece of walking literature, *Wild Wales*. 'It is not only necessary for me to see the sources of the rivers,' Borrow informed his guide, 'but to drink of them, in order that in after times I may be able to harangue about them with a tone of confidence and authority.' The man took Borrow unerringly to three river sources; but he seems to have tricked his client in doing so, for Borrow's compass

ABOVE: In west Wales you can still see river fishermen using the traditional coracle, a round boat light enough to carry on the back.

OPPOSITE: A pause to admire the view during the ascent of the 2,930-ft (893-m) Cader Idris.

directions and description of the source of the Severn in fact match that of the little River Gwarn – a much easier and pleasanter spring for the guide to reach than the boggy quagmire where the Severn actually rises.

No such conmanship for the old man from Dolgellau who took the diarist curate Francis Kilvert (1840–1879) up Cader Idris in 1871. It was a vile day of cloud, rain, mist and high wind, and the guide seemed so slow and decrepit that Kilvert feared the old boy might collapse and have to be carried down to safety. In fact he proved tough enough to get the curate up to the top and down again by way of the Fox's Path, a fearful downward scramble only attempted even today by agile walkers properly shod. The pair dropped 'down, down and out of the cloud into sunshine, all the hills below and the valleys bathed in glorious sunshine – a wonderful and dazzling sight'. The view from the mountain, halfway across Wales, is indeed a breathtaking one. But Kilvert, scribbling his impressions at the Golden Lion in Dolgellau that June evening, had been thoroughly disillusioned by the bad weather and his anxiety about the guide. 'Cader Idris,' he decided, 'is the stoniest, dreariest, most desolate mountain I was ever on ... it is an awful place in a storm. I thought of Moses on Sinai.'

The mightiest of the Welsh mountains are clustered in the National Park of Snowdonia in the north-west corner of Wales. This is slate and schist country, a tumbled geology upthrust into mountain ranges peaking

ABOVE LEFT: Portmeirion, a fantasy village assembled on the Snowdonia coast by Sir Clough Williams-Ellis (1883–1978), famous Welsh architect and landscape designer, out of architectural fragments from every corner of the world.

LEFT: As a contrast to light and frothy Portmeirion, the turrets and walls of Pembroke Castle are grim strength personified.

OPPOSITE: Looking across the Mawddach Estuary to Barmouth.

ABOVE: Welsh industrial heritage celebrated at Llechwedd Slate Caverns, Blaenau Ffestiniog.

at well over 3,000 feet (900 metres). There are cavernous slate mines to explore at Blaenau Ffestiniog, and steam railways to ride. For climbing there are the looming dark mountains at the heart of Snowdonia: the rugged ranges of the Glyders and Carneddau, and towering to the south-west of these the king of them all, the magnificent 3,560-foot (1,085-metre) Snowdon itself. *Yr Wyddfa*, 'the Tomb', the Welsh call it: the giant Rhita Fawr, wearer of a cloak woven of the beards of kings he had killed, lies buried here, slain by the hero Arthur. There are half a dozen ways up Snowdon (including, for faint-hearts, a steam-hauled mountain railway), each giving spectacular views until you top out at the summit. The reward is a view that can stretch up to 250 miles (400 kilometres) on the clearest of days, taking in Wales, England, Scotland and even a far-off glimpse of the Wicklow Hills over the sea in Ireland. Across the Menai Strait from Snowdonia lies the large and beautiful island of Anglesey, a rural area with a strong tradition of Welsh-speaking. Beaumaris Castle, overlooking the Strait in a splendid strategic position, was the last of the mighty Iron Ring of castles built by King Edward I in the 1280s to subdue the Welsh and keep them penned up

in the mountains. But Anglesey is probably best known for the village with the highly improbable name – Llanfairpwllgwyngyllgogerychwyrndrobwllllantysilio-gogogoch.

Non-mountaineers often rate the Welsh Borders the best part of Wales for scenery and atmosphere. Where exactly the borderlands between Wales and England – the Marches is their historic title – begin and end is hard to pinpoint. But the ancient earthwork of Offa's Dyke, a defensive lookout bank built by Offa, King of Mercia between 778 and 796, makes a good rough guide as it wriggles south in approximate tandem with today's political border. You can walk Offa's Dyke on a national trail, 168 miles (270 kilometres) through some of Britain's prime landscape.

The Vale of Clwyd, overlooked by the massive ruins of Denbigh Castle, is a green gem. The Vale of Llangollen to the south is a steeper affair altogether, with the hills closing in and the valleys sprouting crag-gy limestone bluffs. South-west again stand the Berwyns, rounded hills of mudstone, sandstone and shale where you can walk the old droving roads all day and have only yourself for company. The waterfall of Pistyll Rhaeadr, one of the Seven Wonders of Wales,

ABOVE: Examples of the basket-maker's art in woven willow, for sale on the craft stall at the Royal Welsh Show in the mid-Wales market town of Builth Wells.

RIGHT: Up Snowdon the lazy way, by Snowdon Mountain Railway.

white houses, and the handsome old Church of St Andrew. Here one of the strangest episodes in Border history (or mythology) took place during the 15th century – the exorcism of the ghost of Black Vaughan of nearby Hergest Court.

Black Vaughan, beheaded after the Battle of Banbury in 1469, had returned to haunt the Borders. Thirteen good men assembled in St Andrew's at Presteigne to deal with him. Summoned to materialise, Black Vaughan caused all but one of his judges to pass out with terror. But the bravest kept his wits, reduced the sprite to the size of a fly and snapped it safely shut into his snuff-box, which was then thrown into the pond below Black Vaughan's house. Sadly, that did not deter the ghost. Accidentally released 100 years later, Black Vaughan still haunts the area in the guise of a hellish black hound – inspiration for Sir Arthur Conan Doyle, who heard the legend while staying in the area and later wove it into *The Hound of the Baskervilles*.

Further south stand the Black Mountains. In all accuracy they should be called the Black Ridges – four deep valleys, interspersed with five long spines of ridges that rise gradually to the north-west until they spill over in prow-like bluffs. Sunk in the heart of the Black Mountains are the romantic ruins of Llanthony Abbey, visited by thousands every holiday. Few bother to penetrate further up the Vale of Ewyas to find Capel-y-ffin and the ruins of Llanthony Tertia, a monastic church half-completed by the extraordinary 19th-century visionary and eccentric, the Reverend Joseph Lyne. He styled himself Father Ignatius, and tried single-handedly to revive the monastic tradition in late Victorian England. In the 1920s the artist-sculptor Eric Gill bought the monastery and the church ruins, and spent a few years here scandalising the locals with his bohemian lifestyle. The long-backed hills around the Vale of Ewyas are stunningly beautiful, and conceal other river valleys more remote and mysterious, with frescoed churches, hidden ruins and pubs and farms that might have sprung fully fledged from a pre-motor age.

It is the River Wye that returns us to the Severn and to England, winding down from Monmouth through cliffs at first of sandstone and sloped well back, then of limestone and shaped like sheer ramparts. The Wye Valley, thickly wooded, is a lovely place to saunter. It passes the almost complete shell of the Cistercian abbey at Tintern, where the stone tracery of the great windows frames the wooded valley slopes, and reaches the southernmost Border town of Chepstow beneath the ramparts of the oldest stone-built castle in Britain. A final couple of miles and the Wye dissolves itself in the broad salt waters of the Severn Estuary.

ABOVE: The 240-ft (73-m) double fall of Pistyll Rhaeadr in the flanks of the Berwyn Hills.

OPPOSITE: The superb view over the Wye Valley from Symonds Yat.

crashes 240 feet (73 metres) in a double leap at the end of the valley above Llanrhaeadr-ym-Mochnant, 'the church near the waterfall of the stream where pigs are'. George Borrow came here, viewed the tremendous battering power of the waterfall, and produced on the spot (so he said) a translation of an *englyn* he found in the visitor's book at the nearby farmhouse:

*Crychiawg, ewynawg anian-yw y Rhyadr*
*Yn rhuo mal taran;*
*Colofn o dwr, gloyw-dwr glan,*
*Gorwyllt, un lliw ag arian.*
Foaming and frothing from mountainous height,
Roaring like thunder the Rhyadr falls;
Though its silvery splendour the eye may delight,
Its fury the heart of the bravest appals.

Around Montgomery, Offa's Dyke switchbacks like a thrashing dragon tail; likewise above Llanfair Waterdine further south, one of the best-preserved sections of the ancient rampart. At Presteigne there are black-and-

# 5
# HEARTLAND

## WHERE VIBRANT NEW CULTURES
## MEET RUSTIC MIDDLE ENGLAND

ABOVE: With its black-and-white medieval houses, handsome abbey church and narrow alleys leading to the River Avon, the Gloucestershire town of Tewkesbury is one of the most attractive and characterful in England's heartland.

OPPOSITE: The creaky, bowed and heavily timbered houses of Church Lane, flanking the cobbled roadway that leads towards the tall spire of Ledbury's Church of St Michael, present a picture of Herefordshire almost unchanged since medieval times.

HE MIDLANDS OF ENGLAND – who could be sure of locating this sprawling region precisely? A great wheel of country 100 miles (161 kilometres) in diameter, with its hub at Coventry and its rim brushing Wales in the west, Oxford in the south, Cambridge to the east and South Yorkshire to the north. The Heart of England, as its tourist industry likes to remind us, boasts some of the most delightful countryside in Britain. Yet it also contains some of the most uncompromisingly plain urban scenes. It is the land of half-timbered cottages and tower blocks, of country lanes and motorway intersections, of dreaming spires and cooling towers, of lazy rivers and grimy canals; a region where some rustic villages seem hardly to have changed since Shakespeare walked their paths, yet where a quarter of the inhabitants of one large city are of Asian origin.

Although the River Severn forms a natural boundary between Wales and England, it does not actually follow the political border between the two countries. In its lower windings the great tidal river flows through the English soil of Gloucestershire. Most of the county lies on the eastern bank of the Severn; but there is one little enclave left islanded to the west, hard up against Welsh Monmouthshire – the Forest of Dean.

The Forest is a place like nowhere else in Britain. It is a wonderful smother of trees and open common land, occupying some 35 square miles (91 square kilometres) of arrow-headed country between Severn and Wye. Beneath the forest floor run unnumbered coal mine shafts and levels, and the cave-like delvings of iron ore mines. The 'Foresters' – those born within the Forest – are entitled by age-old custom to work the seams as 'freeminers', a tradition and privilege some of them still uphold. As in Hampshire's New Forest, an ancient Court of Verderers administers Forest Law (as it has done since perhaps as long ago as the reign of King Canute) to preserve 'vert and venison' – the flora and fauna of the Forest.

The Verderers may have only a ceremonial function these days, but they symbolise and celebrate the independent-mindedness, the sheer 'otherness' of Forest-born people. The Freeminers, too, have their own Court which meets, like the Verderers, in the 17th-century Speech House (now a noted hotel) at the centre of the Forest. From the Speech House, footpaths, cycleways and bridleways radiate out through the depths of the Forest 'inclosures' – a Sculpture Trail, a trail by ponds and old iron-workings, tree trails, nature trails and trails without theme or purpose, where you can walk all day under the old oaks, sweet chestnuts and hollies on a soft carpet of leaves, seeing nobody. A rare solitude.

The Severn winds on inland, tidal as far as the city of Gloucester and a potent influence on dwellers along its flood plain. A glance at the map shows few settlements

within a mile of the river as it snakes its course between Gloucester and Tewkesbury. There is a good reason for that: each February or March, meltwaters coming down from the Welsh mountains swell the Severn until it bursts its banks and floods the surrounding countryside. It is a spectacular display of sovereignty: the streets of Gloucester and Tewkesbury brim, country lanes disappear under fathoms of water, houses are islanded, villages cut off. Willows, hedge-tops and telephone poles stick up disconsolately from the waters. Regulars struggle by canoe and waders to the Boat Inn on the riverbank at Ashleworth, and drink their beer standing in 18 inches of water. At last the floods subside, sandbags are removed from front doorsteps, cattle tread the sodden fields to mud, and a tideline of sticks and tatters of plastic is left hanging at head height in the riverside trees as a memento of King Severn's annual visitation.

Eccentric customs are alive and well and living in Gloucestershire. At Cooper's Hill near Brockworth on the outskirts of Gloucester, thousands turn out each Spring Bank Holiday to watch daredevil participants chase rolling cheeses down the breakneck slope of the hill. Collisions are frequent, tumbles inevitable, injuries far from rare – all for the honour and glory of catching the cheeses. It is the same spirit that used to enliven the village of Oxenton, not far from Tewkesbury, when in the depths of winter they would set a wheel ablaze and

ABOVE: Cannop Ponds, rich in wildlife, lie hidden in the heart of the Forest of Dean.

RIGHT: The River Severn bursts its banks in a springtime flood at Worcester.

roll it down the slope of Oxenton Knoll. Good or ill fortune for the village during the coming year depended on which way the wheel rolled when it reached the bottom of the hill.

Gloucester boasts a beautiful Norman cathedral, rebuilt and embellished in the 14th century as pilgrims flocked to the tomb of King Edward II, popularly regarded as a saint after his disgusting murder in 1327 in nearby Berkeley Castle. Fan-vaulted, filled with notable tombs, Gloucester is one of the 'Three Cathedrals' – the other two are its neighbours at

Worcester and Hereford – whose choirs share a famous yearly choral festival. Worcester Cathedral, superbly sited on the bank of the River Severn, has as a backdrop the Malvern Hills, a 9-mile (14-kilometre) chain of miniature Alps that rises steeply from the flat Worcestershire farmlands. The Malverns, source of many springs of clear spa water, are made of the oldest rock in Britain, a dense granite. Around the turn of the 20th century the composer Edward Elgar (1857–1934) lived for a time at Malvern Wells in the shadow of the hills. He loved them, and drew inspiration from them

ABOVE: Glorious gardens and mellow architecture combine at Abbotswood in the Cotswold village of Lower Swell.

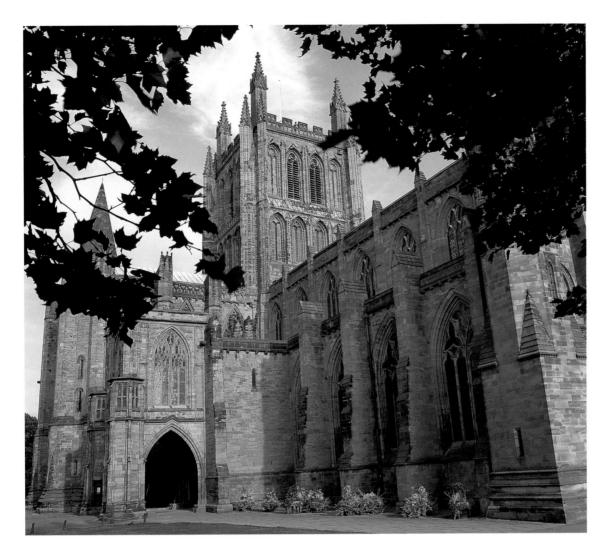

OPPOSITE: Humpy spine of the
Malvern Hills, inspiration for
the music of Sir Edward Elgar.

LEFT: Hereford Cathedral
houses Mappa Mundi,
a wonderful 13th-century
chart of the world.

for the 'Enigma Variations', his cello concerto, and much other wonderful music. An exhilarating footpath runs the whole switchback length of the Malverns' ridge, with views far into Wales and over to the Cotswold Hills.

The third of the Three Cathedrals, Hereford, has a solid Norman heart, overlain with later elaborations. Displayed here in its own purpose-built centre is the fabulous Mappa Mundi, a unique map of the world as conjectured by its creator Richard de Bello in 1289. Admiring the workmanship, the interleaving of known fact and historico-mythical depiction (the tented encampment of Alexander the Great, the vortex-like labyrinth of King Minos in Crete, the Golden Fleece) and flights of sheer fancy (unicorns and centaurs on the plains of Africa, a Far Eastern sciapod snoozing in the shade of his own foot), one sees unfolding the energy, voraciousness and power to marvel of an educated mind in the era before the seafaring adventurers of the 15th and 16th centuries put some factual flesh on the bones of speculation.

South-west of Hereford runs the aptly named Golden Valley, a shallow basin of rich farmland set at regular intervals with superb medieval churches. At Peterchurch it is Norman architecture on a Saxon groundplan, with far older Christian connections. Legend says that Peter and Paul, en route to Spain by ship, were blown off course by a terrific gale. Pitching up in Britain, the two saints put the misadventure to good use by embarking on a preaching tour. St Peter reached the Golden Valley alone, and prepared the waters at Peterchurch for baptisms by catching a giant carp in the River Dore and slipping it into the church well with a gold chain round its neck. Until quite recently the Welsh maintained the custom of keeping a fish in the baptismal well.

Further down the valley stands Abbey Dore, whose soaring Romanesque choir and transepts – still in use for parish worship – were once part of a great Cistercian monastic church. And out beyond the foot of the valley is the glory of the Herefordshire school of religious carving, the small sandstone church of St Mary and St David at Kilpeck. This must be the most eye-wideningly bizarre,

ABOVE: Stream valleys
known as 'batches' furrow
the flanks of the Long Mynd
in Shropshire.

surrealistic church art in Britain – a close-packed riot of saints and soldiers, troll-like evangelists, Green Men, loose women, dogs, ducks, demons and dragons, all created by 12th-century master carvers in a kind of ecstasy of what can best be described as devout paganism.

Herefordshire runs north into Shropshire, county of memorable hill ranges. Clun Forest stands out west, and the broken outlines of the much-quarried Clee Hills to the east. The Clee Hills are often overlooked or bypassed, but there are fine walks up their sandstone flanks to their volcanic basalt peaks, and Norman churches tucked away in the farmlands round about. North-west of Clee stands the uplift of Wenlock Edge, a long double ridge of limestone, with the secret valley of Hopedale running out of sight in the trough between the two rounded waves of the Edge.

From Wenlock Edge you look west across to the jagged volcanic peaks of the Caradoc Hills. Stories say that this was where the Celtic chief Caradoc or Caractacus was captured in a battle with the Romans, before being sent to Rome in chains. Beyond the Caradocs rises the great whaleback of the Long Mynd, its steep sides cut with 'batches' or stream valleys, its smooth top rolling away towards Montgomery and the Welsh border. Up there you walk in a breezy, top-of-the-world landscape, over dour moorland towards the stark outlines of the Stiperstones that are seen piercing the skyline from miles away. These are outcrops of quartzite 500 million years old, weirdly shaped and spicily named – Shepherd's Rock, Scattered Rock, the Devil's Chair, Manstone Rock and Cranberry Rock. Strange dark

ABOVE: The Devil's Chair,
Stiperstones: Old Nick himself
occupies the outcrop on misty
nights, so it's said.

LEFT: Looking over the
plains of Cheshire from
Alderley Edge.

legends attach to them. The Devil's Chair is really a heap of stones let slip from the Devil's apron: he was carrying them from Ireland to block up Hell Gutter when his apron strings came loose. If mist descends on the Stiperstones (as it frequently does), you can be sure that the Devil is concealed up there, sitting in his chair waiting for the stones to sink back into the ground. When they do, England will be lost. Don't be near the Stiperstones three nights before Christmas – that is the night that Wild Edric the Saxon comes to meet the other ghosts of Shropshire and to mourn the loss of his fairy wife. He met her out hunting at the stones, loved her, and lost her to a broken promise. Such are the stories that swirl around the Stiperstones, as thick as moor mist.

Eastwards from Shropshire curve the counties of the north Midlands, Cheshire, Staffordshire, Derbyshire, Nottinghamshire and Leicestershire: fertile plains rising to high country of limestone dales and gritstone moors – the southern outliers of the Pennine Hills – before falling away again into the rich rolling acres of the 'Galloping Shires', the archetypal fox-hunting country of Middle England. Here in the wide, flattish fields of Nottinghamshire and Leicestershire, many of the hedges are still laid by hand as they used to be down the centuries – a highly specialised skill, and one that results in what every artist-craftsman longs to achieve – something both beautiful and useful. Neither beautiful nor useful, but good dirty fun, is the Hare Pie Scramble and Bottle Kicking contested in the Leicestershire village of Hallaton each Easter Monday – another of those wildly eccentric British traditions that combines arcane rules, a plentiful allowance of rough play, and the consumption of vast quantities of ale.

From the lake-pocked plateau of central Cheshire the ground slopes up to the sandstone crags of Alderley Edge. Thickly wooded, a little jewel of remoteness in the middle of a belt of densely settled Manchester commuterdom, Alderley Edge is steeped in mystery. The entire outcrop is riddled and honeycombed with tunnels, driven deep under the Edge by centuries of iron and copper ore mining. Maybe it was these that gave rise to the famous legend ...

A local farmer, riding over Alderley Edge to sell his milk-white mare at the fair, is stopped by a wild-looking stranger. Can he buy the horse, please? No, says the farmer – someone at the fair will be sure to offer a better price. But they do not. Returning home grumpily with the unsold mare that night, the farmer is once more accosted by the stranger. This time he agrees to the sale, whereupon master and horse are led by the strange purchaser through a pair of iron gates into a

cave deep in the earth. Here they find a crowd of sleeping men-at-arms, each with a milk-white horse slumbering beside him – all but one. King Arthur and his knights, says the wizard – for such he is – all waiting until England shall have dire need of them to wake and ride to the rescue. Gently he leads the mare to the one horseless knight, and she sinks down beside him in an enchanted slumber.

The wizard leads the farmer on into a treasure room scattered with gold and jewels. 'Come,' says he, 'help yourself to a fair price for your horse.' The farmer has no sooner crammed his pockets with coins and precious stones than he finds himself back on the road, free to walk home with his unlooked-for fortune.

To the east rises the district called The Peak District, where the light, flowery limestone uplands of the White Peak and the dour dark gritstone of the Dark Peak moors give edge to one another and to the characteristic drystone walls, small field barns and long house-and-byre conglomerate farmstead buildings. From the north Staffordshire town of Leek the high, lonely moors lead east to the beautiful Derbyshire cleft of Dovedale. Here a hill stream has carved out a dale full of limestone crags and pinnacles, a famous beauty

ABOVE: Whether done with wheat straw or reed stalks, the rural art of thatching has never died out in the face of competition from slate and stone. Thatched roofs are warm in winter, cool in summer, watertight and attractive. They should only need renewing every 30 years or so. 'Give her a good hat of reed,' say the Norfolk thatchers, 'and she'll last a working life.'

OPPOSITE: Wooded slopes rising to limestone outcrops, and a wide view beyond: a characteristic vista of the Peak District.

spot whose natural features carry romantic names: the Twelve Apostles, Tissington Spires, Jacob's Ladder, Reynard's Cave, Lover's Leap. It was from Lover's Leap that Dean Langton of Clougher fell to his death in 1761, along with his horse. His lady companion also fell, but her long hair caught in the branches of a tree on the way down and pulled her up short. She was rescued, hysterical but unharmed.

Buxton became a highly fashionable spa resort during the 18th century, and retains an air of well-heeled dignity along with its crescents, squares and fine Edwardian opera house. Bakewell to the east is a neat, friendly little town with a famous delicacy (Bakewell Pudding, a tooth-tinglingly sweet mixture of jam, custard and almonds) to tempt visitors. There are great country houses in superb parkland: Chatsworth, the

Palladian mansion of the Dukes of Devonshire, and Hardwick Hall, whose imperious Elizabethan chatelaine, the Countess of Shrewsbury (better known as Bess of Hardwick), accorded herself all the honour and glory appropriate to a queen. But it is the dales with their deep-cut valleys – Miller's Dale, for example, or the secret cleft of Lathkill Dale near Bakewell – that are the real pride and glory of the Peak District.

Nottinghamshire clings on to a few remnants of the once-mighty Sherwood Forest of Robin Hood. The county boasts one of Britain's most delightful minster churches at Southwell. Here the medieval stone-masons gave their imagination free rein – especially in the 13th-century Chapter House, where Green Men, mermen, pigs, dogs, saints and hares gambol among foliage carved with exquisite naturalism. The ancient and painstaking art of lacemaking is still kept alive in the county city of Nottingham, where the lace centre opposite the castle and the Museum of Costume and Textiles display superb examples.

Leicestershire's broad acres lead towards the city of Leicester at the centre of the county – not a visually attractive place, but home to a tremendously vibrant Asian community. A quarter of the city's population is of Asian origin, integrated but still retaining their distinctive, primarily Hindu way of life. The Sikh community's Guru Nanak Gurdwara temple, and the great temple of the Jains recently built by craftsmen brought from India for the purpose, are superb. The streets come alive in November, a kaleidoscope of colourful saris, lights, jewellery and silks as the festivals of Navratri and Diwali are celebrated with all comers welcome.

There is more cross-cultural mixing and magic in the city of Birmingham and its satellite region of the Black Country. Together they form Britain's second largest city, essentially a vast agglomeration of small industrial villages, each proud of its own local traditions, that grew up during the Industrial Revolution. Brummies (Birmingham inhabitants) don't do things by halves. Those who bother to penetrate the unlovely suburbs and motorway rings as far as the city centre will find extravagant architecture of outlandish shape and giant size jammed exuberantly together with brash modern sculptures and fine old brick canal offices and bridges. Birmingham calls itself, with typical irony, the Venice of England – and certainly it is proud of possessing a greater mileage of waterways than Italy's city of canals. It also possesses literally hundreds of Asian eating houses, famous for their inexpensive and spicily delicious curries, another beneficial spin-off from the city's lively immigrant cultures. To conclude a visit to Birmingham without enjoying a meal in one of the curry houses in the city's so-called 'Balti Triangle' is to miss half the fun.

South of the West Midlands you slip into Warwickshire and the county of William Shakespeare (1564–1616). Woods and hedged fields characterise the landscape, along with ancient green lanes and fine red brick country houses. Shakespeare-related buildings – his birthplace, the houses of his daughters, the schoolroom he attended – are handsomely maintained in Stratford-upon-Avon, where millions visit the Bard's tomb in the pale stone Church of the Holy Trinity on the banks of the River Avon. Not far away are Shakespeare's mother's half-timbered house in the

LEFT: The timber-framed house on Henley Street, Stratford-upon-Avon, where William Shakespeare was born on 23 April 1564.

OVERLEAF: Standing high and mighty on a curve of the River Avon, Warwick Castle symbolises the pride and power of the medieval Earls of Warwick.

village of Wilmcote, and the brick farmhouse in the hamlet of Shottery, which was the childhood home of the playwright's wife Anne Hathaway.

South again to the Cotswolds, those gently undulating cushions of hills with their unexpectedly steep valleys. The field walls, barns, churches and houses of Cotswold are built of the sometimes silvery, sometimes creamy oolitic limestone that underlies the hills. The drystone walls of the Cotswold fields have been neglected over recent decades; but now efforts are being made, partly with volunteer labour, to bring them into repair again. Watching a skilled waller mending a breach in a Cotswold stone wall, assessing the limestone slabs to work out exactly where they should be laid for maximum effectiveness, is always a delight.

Warwickshire, Gloucestershire and Oxfordshire meet to the north-east of the dignified Regency spa resort of Cheltenham. From here the Cotswolds trend east through a broad scatter of delectable towns and villages – Winchcombe with nearby medieval Sudeley Castle, the twin Tudor villages of Stanton and Stanway, Bourton-on-the-Water, where pretty little footbridges

carry you across the hurrying Windrush River, and gorgeous Chipping Campden with its carefully preserved air of prosperous timelessness. Down in south Gloucestershire, where the hills tumble towards Somerset and Mendip, there are tall old mill buildings in the fast-flowing stream valleys around Stroud. Up in south Warwickshire near Shipston-on-Stour the Cotswolds lift and broaden into wide upland sheepwalks and cornlands. And over into Oxfordshire they divide and spread, the stone of the buildings and field walls becoming steadily more gold, as they dip down to the Thames Valley and the towers and spires of Oxford.

Mellow Oxford takes time to get to know. There is just too much to take in and appreciate on a single visit. This is Britain's longest-established place of education, a city built up with layer upon layer of culture and tradition, and of patronage by the great and the good. All has coalesced to produce the world's finest and most civilised seat of learning (*pace* Cambridge), rich with treasures of memorable medieval architecture that only several days on foot around the city can show you.

# 6

# FENS AND FLATLANDS: EAST ANGLIA

## THE SLEEPY CORNER THAT IS FULL OF SURPRISES

ABOVE: Weeping willows overhang the River Cam at Cambridge.

OPPOSITE: Creeks in the Norfolk salt-marshes at Cley-next-the-Sea fill and dry according to the tide.

W HAT EAST ANGLIA IS – huge skies over flat marshes, flints in chalky clay soil, church towers in giant fields, wildfowl in winter by the hundred thousand, a sideways air of not being quite up with the times – everyone senses. But no one can define exactly *where* East Anglia is. All that lies within that great inlet-slashed wheel of land clamped to the eastern flank of England, certainly; all that one understands by 'Fenland', too, and everything too far east and out of the way to be reached by the hydra-headed motorways striking out of London. East Anglia takes its definition from mood and atmosphere rather than from geography. There are no dramatic landforms, no mountains or grand skyline formations on which to hang the region's character. Like wine, an appreciation of East Anglia matures slowly. It eases into your affections in the way that its coastline eases into the North Sea: gently, and by subtle degrees.

Subtlety is the key to Cambridge, sister city of Oxford, her rival and yardstick. Oxford comes at your senses directly, making you gasp in admiration at first contact. Cambridge lets you come at her, through that peculiarly thick and dreamy fen air. Colours are muted, sounds muffled, shapes softened. It is as if a miasma of the million acres of old Fenland, sodden watery peatlands, still hangs in the air of the city.

There is a slowness about Cambridge, partly to do with the sense of timelessness engendered by the leisurely bicycling undergraduates, partly owing to the numbers of visitors who stroll about the place. Cambridge is a walking and bicycling city, small enough to be got round in a day, packed with enough of beauty and interest to be explored for a month. Since water – in the atmosphere, and under the bridges – is such an integral part of Cambridge, a good way to approach the city is from the south, walking the field path beside the River Granta (its name changes to the River Cam, some insist, upon entering Cambridge) through the lush green pastures of Grantchester Meadows. It was in the village of Grantchester that the poet Rupert Brooke (1887–1915) lodged from 1909 to 1911, catching perfectly that seductive undergraduate laziness in his poem *The Old Vicarage, Grantchester*:

> I only know that you may lie
> Day long and watch the Cambridge sky,
> And, flower-lulled in sleepy grass,
> Hear the cool lapse of hours pass,
> Until the centuries blend and blur
> In Grantchester, in Grantchester...

Undergraduates punt up the Granta (or Cam) today, just as they did in Rupert Brooke's era, into the city and along The Backs, those wide green spaces – half lawns,

half fields – that fringe the river as it undulates north past the colleges in the heart of the city. Cambridge University was founded by disaffected Oxford scholars around the turn of the 13th century, and its colleges were built one by one during the following centuries as money was donated for them by rich men, royalty, religious orders or trade guilds. A punter or stroller up along The Backs passes Peterhouse, founded in 1284 and the oldest of the Cambridge colleges; the Tudor glories of Queen's; King's, with its world-renowned chapel rich in Gothic fan-vaulting and Tudor stained glass; the Jacobean college of Clare, where a beautiful

bridge of 1639 spans the river; Trinity, in whose Nevile's Court the speed of sound was calculated by Isaac Newton (he stamped his foot and timed the echo); the pinnacled Bridge of Sighs leading to St John's, William Wordsworth's college; and medieval Magdalene, the northernmost college. These are architectural, historical and cultural riches unrivalled (*pace* Oxford) by any other medieval city centre in Britain.

The fen country that stretches away north of Cambridge would hardly be recognised in its modern guise by the fenmen who eked a living as wild-fowlers, eel-trappers, sedge- and reed-cutters and peat-diggers at the time the university colleges were being built. Before the Earl of Bedford brought the Dutch engineer Cornelius Vermuyden across to Cambridgeshire in 1630, Fenland was a truly wild place of reedbeds, sedgy marshes and snaking, flood-prone rivers, a fever-ridden no-man's-land where lonely monastic settlements and their isolated towns stood clear of the water on low islands of glacial rubble. The National Trust preserves a few acres of the real old fenland at Wicken Fen, north-east of Cambridge, a bushy and vari-coloured mosaic of carr woodland, open fen, water and meadow, bursting with wildlife.

monks; also to the drainers' influence, riding as they do like great ships above green seas of corn and root leaves. And the artificiality of the land itself attests the changes: roads and rivers are cut strict and straight, looking on the map as if they have all been raked to the north-east by some gigantic harrow. Down on the ground you observe that they run 20 feet (6 metres) above the surrounding fields, whose level peat has shrunken away and fallen as it dried. These great hedgeless fenland fields look sinister and threatening when the wind blows the peat dust in dark clouds round the solitary farms. They

ABOVE: One of the greatest thrills a bird-watcher in Fenland can hope for is to hear a strange booming noise echoing through the reed beds – the territorial cry of the very rare and elusive bittern. These speckled brown cousins of the heron camouflage themselves among the reeds by standing motionless with their necks and bills pointed skywards, a stance almost impossible to pick out among the brown vertical lines of the reed stalks.

LEFT: Lush ancient fenland preserved by the National Trust at Wicken Fen National Nature Reserve, a few miles north of Cambridge.

Vermuyden and Bedford invested venture capital in cutting two ruler-straight parallel rivers, the Old and New Bedford Rivers, for 20 miles (32 kilometres) northeast across the Fens. With these they drained the land and controlled the river and sea surges that had so often inundated it. Fenland became what it is today, a mightily productive disc of flat, Grade 1 farmland where the potatoes, cabbages, turnips and onions spring from the black peat-rich soil as if they were Jack's magic beansprouts. The monastery churches and abbey remains at sites such as Crowland, Ramsey, Ely and Thorney bear witness to the power and prosperity of the

take on a haunting beauty on a fine spring evening after rain, when the low sun turns thousands of narrow furrows into ribs of glinting fire as they converge to a vanishing point on the horizon.

Until they get a proper focus on the attractions that are wrapped up in the strangeness of Fenland, people tend to dismiss the region as 'a million acres of spuds'. And those with untuned antennae stigmatise the county of Essex as an unsightly and maybe dangerous eastward excrescence on the backside of London. This view is generally held by people who know Essex only from rushing through it in a car as quickly as possible, in

order to get to gentle and pastoral Suffolk and Norfolk. Certainly there is an ugly entrance corridor for anyone travelling out of London into the county by way of sprawling overspill towns such as Romford, Brentwood and Basildon. Southend-on-Sea (or, more accurately, Southend-on-Estuary) is the time-honoured seaside resort of London's East Enders; its famous mile-long (1.6-kilometre-long) pier, sticking far out above the muddy waters of the Thames, makes a fine promenading stroll. Beyond Southend you will find an unsuspected beauty in the lost-and-forgotten farmlands way out

east, in tiny weatherboarded hamlets like Paglesham Churchend and Barling, out where the coast is cut into a complicated maze of islands by muddy tidal creeks and rivers. Here, along the Crouch and Roach and Blackwater, the sailing boat is king. Brent geese, redshank and plover feed along the tidelines: it is serious bird-watchers' heaven. In all the huge acreage of the blunt-faced Dengie Peninsula between the Crouch and the Blackwater there is not a single town – only a handful of small villages and a sprinkle of farms as lonely as any in Fenland. Yet these long miles of seawall and cornfields, where you can walk all day and see nobody, are only an hour from London.

A little further north and you are into the mazy sidewindings of the Blackwater Estuary with its handsome salt-making port of Maldon, its big swathes of grazing marshes, saltings and mud flats, and its little causeway islands. Just downriver from Maldon, the bushy few acres of Northey Island saw one of the

ABOVE: A yacht under full sail cuts up the River Blackwater towards the port of Maldon in north Essex.

ABOVE: The roots of morris dancing probably go way back into pagan fertility rituals, but nowadays a politely sanitised version sees handkerchiefs a-flick and leg bells a-jingle in one of rural Britain's most evocative traditions.

OPPOSITE TOP: As a young man John Constable worked in his father's flour mill at Flatford; later he was to incorporate the scene into his best-known landscape painting, The Hay-wain (1821).

OPPOSITE BOTTOM: Suffolk is rich in timber-framed medieval buildings such as the 15th-century Swan Hotel.

most ferocious battles fought on English soil, in AD 991 when the Danes were in full invasive flood along the east coast. Why local Saxon warlord Brihtnoth allowed a strong party of Danish raiders to cross the causeway from Northey Island to the mainland, when he had them safely penned up there, has never been properly explained. He paid for the misjudgement with his life, and the lives of hundreds of his followers. 'Keenly they warred,' lamented the contemporary bardic composer of The Battle of Maldon:

> ... Burst the shield's edge, as the hauberk sang
> A grisly war song ... The seamen advanced,
> Wrathful in fight; the spear oft pierced
> The body of the doomed one ... Warriors fell,
> Weary with wounds; slaughter fell on earth ...

Beyond Northey Island, two more islands lie in the fairway of the Blackwater Estuary: little Osea Island, and the oval bulk of Mersea Island where you can enjoy locally caught oysters. Nearby are the lonely, seabird-haunted Tollesbury Marshes. The improbable scarlet blob of a retired lightship, moored in one of the muddy creeks, enlivens the sombre greens and greys of

the marshes. Inland Essex is as compelling as the coast, and as undervalued by travellers. Once beyond the influence of London, there are nuggets of peaceful countryside sheltering some of the most attractive towns and villages in England. Here stands Thaxted with its tottery 15th-century Guildhall and its glorious church (Gustav Holst put in a stint as organist). Not far away are Saffron Walden, whose streets are lined with fine medieval houses colour-washed or brick-nogged, and historic Colchester, the oldest town in Britain, with an impressive array of Roman remains. The great early medieval barns at Cressing Temple near Braintree are among the finest in Europe, great wooden 'Cathedrals of the Harvest', each massive roof supported on a skeleton forest of rough-cut timber. Coggeshall, on the road to Colchester, boasts more beautifully carved old buildings: and here the Grange Barn (haunted, some say) dates back to 1140, making it the oldest barn still standing in Europe.

The barrier between the northern border of Essex and the southern boundary of Suffolk is a watery one. The River Stour winds a leisurely 40 miles (60 kilometres) between the neighbouring counties to the head of its estuary. There it broadens eastward for another 12 miles (20 kilometres), to meet its sister River Orwell and the sea between the ancient Essex port of Harwich and the high-technology Suffolk dock town of Felixstowe. The lower part of the river's journey, around Dedham and Flatford, runs through the countryside so often painted by John Constable (1776–1837). Scenes from his great landscape paintings – Flatford Mill, Dedham Lock and Mill, The Hay-wain – are still easily recognisable. The Stour is a delectable river, slow and lazy, and some of Suffolk's prettiest old wool towns line its banks.

In the early Middle Ages Suffolk and Norfolk, the two neighbouring heartland counties of East Anglia, had the densest population in Britain, thanks to the excellence of their rolling grassland plains for sheep-grazing. It was wool-selling, and later wool-weaving under the guidance of refugee immigrants from the Low Countries across the North Sea, that made East Anglia rich. The wool merchants built handsomely for themselves and their workers, solid houses with heavily carved beams, their walls decorated with the relief plasterwork known as pargetting, their brick chimneys tall and twisted, their roofs thatched or sealed with red earthenware tiles. The rich men and their associates built other fine structures, too: dignified guildhalls for the trade's various unions, as well as barns and mills. The timber frames of these buildings generally shifted shape during their first decades, settling and hardening into crooked attitudes. But they were built to last – and

they did, as charming small towns such as Cavendish, Clare, Long Melford, Sudbury and Nayland bear witness. The pearl supreme, Lavenham – capital of the Suffolk wool trade for the two boom centuries that culminated in the Tudor era – stands on the wolds a few miles north of the Stour Valley. To walk Lavenham's streets past oversailing upper storeys, extravagantly leaning wall frames, carved doorposts and ancient dormer windows peering out like owls' eyes from mellow tiled roofs is to step back in time. Showpiece stars here include the black-and-white Swan Hotel (every overseas visitor's dream archetype of the 'olde Englishe inne') and the great Guildhall of 1529, exuberantly carved, with slender mullioned windows.

The wool merchants built fine houses, and they also paid for the building or enhancement of parish

churches all over East Anglia. Suffolk and Norfolk enjoy a glorious treasury of beautiful medieval churches. The jewel among those along the Stour Valley is probably Holy Trinity at Long Melford, a vast building on a rise of ground with some of England's best 15th-century stained glass and some wonderful stone carving and flint flushwork.

There are splendid country house mansions dotted around Suffolk. Long Melford has two: turreted Melford Hall and moated Kentwell Hall, both brick-built around the time that Queen Elizabeth I came to the throne. Ickworth House near Bury St Edmunds is a later creation, a wonderful folly consisting of an enormous rotunda flanked by long wings which was built on the inspiration of Frederick Hervey, 4th Earl of Bristol and Bishop of Londonderry, at the turn of the 19th century. Hervey was one of those uninhibited eccentrics thrown up by the English landed classes at the time – he had a whole series of follies built for himself on the Antrim cliffs in Ulster, supported a number

ABOVE: What the mechanical hedge-slasher can never achieve: the creation of a living, natural barrier by one man's skill and physical effort.

RIGHT: A rare sight these days, but one which causes all the cars to stop and all the gateways to fill with wide-eyed onlookers – a pair of heavy horses ploughing a field. Before tractors began appearing on the farms between the wars, a skilled horse ploughman would reckon to plough a furrow from one side of a field to the other without deviating more than a couple of inches from a dead straight line.

of mistresses, and liked to have himself carried around Rome in a palanquin.

Most of inland Suffolk is still very rural, and closely bound up with agriculture – some of it the large-scale, prairie-style agribusiness of grain barons, but much still revolving around the family farm. The land flows with the smooth slow rhythms of heavy clay, and Suffolk people can seem the same way in thought and conversation. 'Silly Suffolk' is the catchphrase. There's nothing silly in the characteristic deliberate stolidity of born-and-bred Suffolk rural workers. Those who are lucky enough not to be sealed deaf-and-dumb in the cab of an agricultural machine monster still take a pride in laying a hedge or ploughing a furrow carefully, properly, as their parents used to do.

In *Akenfield*, his masterly depiction through oral testimony of life in the Suffolk village of Charsfield, Ronald Blythe records one of his interviewees recalling how 'the men forgot that they were the farmer's fields when they were ploughing and planting them, and decked and tended them most perfectly.' One farmer, enraged because his tired workforce had knocked off early during one harvest, kept them all standing in the farmyard for half an hour the next day, every man silent and terrified in case he should be sacked. Then the farmer curtly ordered them back to work. 'The men didn't hurry their harvest; they made a masterpiece of it. It was their defiance.'

The Suffolk coast rises from the Essex border at the confluence of the Stour and Orwell, a convex curve trending north-east and then north for some 50 miles (80 kilometres) to its meeting with Norfolk between Lowestoft and Great Yarmouth. This is no sand-and-sunshine holiday coast. It is a pebbly strand, solid shingle for mile after mile, penetrated by the muddy, bird-haunted estuaries of the rivers Deben, Alde, Blyth and Waveney. In 40 miles (64 kilometres) of coast only Aldeburgh and Southwold are settlements of any size. Two delicacies peculiar to this coast are the oysters grown in the Butley River and sold in the characterful old port of Orford, and the far-famed Adnams Bitter brewed at Southwold and drunk wherever two or three discerning beer enthusiasts are gathered together.

The Suffolk coast is lonely country, marshy behind the sea defences that run for much of its length, stony on the seaward side. Martello towers stand out on the shore at regular intervals, stark relics of the years when Napoleon's domination of Europe posed a real invasion threat to this remote coast. There are concrete gun emplacements and observation posts of 1940 vintage, too, reminders of the continued vulnerability of these exposed beaches. This is the native coast of one of

Britain's greatest 20th-century composers, Benjamin Britten (1913–1976). He loved the Suffolk shingle and marshland, and wove the sigh of wind in seawall grasses and the rush and suck of sea on pebbles into *Curlew River*, *Peter Grimes*, *Noye's Fludde*, and others of his works.

Starkest and most haunting of all is the great 10-mile (16-kilometre) shingle spit of Orford Ness. The spit runs due south from Aldeburgh, then makes a sharp turn to the south-west, like a bent arm. At the bulge of the elbow lies the Ness itself, wind-whipped and bleak. Rare shingle plants like the glorious pink sea pea hug the storm ridges, co-existing with breeding seabirds

ABOVE: The oval-shaped Martello tower at Shingle Street is one of a string along the Suffolk coast, legacy of early 19th-century English fears of invasion by the forces of Napoleon Bonaparte.

LEFT: By 1825 the avocet had disappeared as a breeding bird from the UK, hounded to extinction for the beauty of its feathers and eggs. But flooding of the Low Countries polders during WWII forced these graceful wading birds to look for alternative breeding grounds. Small numbers began to nest at Minsmere and Havergate Island on the Suffolk coast. Since then a thriving colony has built up and because of this success the RSPB has adopted the avocet as its symbol.

ABOVE: Harvest on a big farm
in pre-mechanisation days
was a labour-intensive
business, with dozens of
men required to stook up
the sheaves and pitchfork
them into the wagons for
transportation to the barn.
Nowadays one man and
his machine can do the lot
by themselves.

RIGHT: A very skilled job
(though a cold and wet one)
that is still carried on in
isolated pockets of the
Norfolk Broads and Fens –
the harvesting of thatching
reeds from carefully
managed reed beds.

such as the roseate and little tern, with foxes and voles,
with wading birds. The spit also holds grim black observation towers and pagoda-shaped bomb-testing buildings, legacy of the 80 years during which the Ministry
of Defence owned Orford Ness and used it for secret bal-
listic and radar experiments. The MoD sold the Ness to
the National Trust in 1993; now the shingle spit with
its birds, plants, animals and strange atmosphere, its
silence and other-worldliness, is relished by the tiny
parties of explorers permitted to wander there.

The neighbouring county of Norfolk is almost an
island, so closely is its perimeter defined by water. The
wheel-rim curve of the North Sea forms the coast, and
the Waveney and Little Ouse rivers define the inland barrier beside which Norfolk marches with Suffolk for the
best part of 100 miles (161 kilometres). Here is the classic
eastern chalk-and-flint country, of deep clay worked over
the centuries by ploughmen so stolid that they became a
byword for slow dependability – 'Norfolk dumplings', reli-
able, unimaginative and as steady as a rock.

Of all the East Anglian counties Norfolk is the least rushed, the most time-suspended. Here are small red-brick and flint country towns like Reepham and North Walsham, and rural villages such as Aslacton with its Saxon church tower, or Binham with its magnificent priory ruins, or Waxham out on the coast where the Great Barn stands under a vast thatched roof. There are a great number of fine halls and big country houses in Norfolk – Blickling and Holkham in particular – witness to the prosperity that wool brought to the area during the Middle Ages. But the East Anglian sheepwalks have been under the plough for many centuries now. Broad swathes of flinty farmland stretch to the horizon, rolling with a gentle rise and fall. Crumbling clay cliffs hem the land in an 80-mile (130-kilometre) arc.

In Norwich the county possesses one of Britain's most appealing small cities. Norwich boasts a 1000-year-old market, some characterful pubs, a fine river frontage along the Wensum ... and 32 churches. Cream of the crop must be Norwich Cathedral itself. In the nave,

stonework soars beautifully carved 100 feet (30 metres) into the air. Green Men grin and leer from the foliage of roof bosses in the cloisters. A dignified Jesus Christ is bullied to his death across the exquisitely painted panels of the 14th-century Despenser Reredos.

East of Norwich stretches Broadland, low-lying country founded on peat beds and dappled with the lake-like fleets of water known as the Norfolk Broads. These days a favoured cruising and yachting ground for freshwater sailors, the Broads are flooded medieval peat pits, excavated for fuel. During the centuries of abandonment that followed their digging, the old hollows filled with water. Marshmen joined them up by cutting interconnecting channels. A whole way of life came into being, founded on wild-fowling, fishing and reed-cutting. Reed and sedge are still cut by hand around How Hill to provide roofing materials for the thatcher. The wildlife of the Norfolk Broads developed into a rich mosaic – butterflies, water birds and insects, wild flowers and trees. But by the late 20th century pollution from diesel oil,

ABOVE: Colourfully striped 'tilts' or awnings shelter the stalls of Norwich's 1000-year-old market.

agricultural run-off and sewage treatment had turned the Broads into sadly sterile brown soups. Now conservationists are fighting back. Sanctuaries such as Ranworth and Hickling Broads and Horsey Mere have been created for the benefit of warblers, flycatchers, bearded tits, marsh harriers, reed buntings, water plants, insects and trees. They have re-established the bittern, the shy booming bird that haunts the reed beds, and protected the habitat of the giant yellow swallowtail, a butterfly as large and beautiful as an exotic bird. Such species throve here long before man and his petrol fumes, oil slicks, agrichemicals, water extraction and general 'couldn't-care-lessness' set about changing their worlds.

The glory of Norfolk is its astonishing heritage of parish churches, the richest collection of any county in Britain, started back in the mists of Saxon time and continued through endowment by rich wool-masters

up until Tudor times and the new puritanism. Tilney All Saints and Walsoken in extreme west Norfolk have wonderful Norman work; at Binham Priory the Norman architectural style actually turns into Early English between one end of the church and the other, its monkish builders having incorporated the new fashion while they were in the process of construction.

At Blakeney on the north Norfolk coast the church with its hammerbeam roof is dedicated to St Nicholas, patron saint of seafarers. It has two towers – a conventional west tower, and at the north-east corner a slender 50-foot (15-metre) additional tower from which to shine a light for the benefit of benighted sailors and marsh travellers. There are giant and elaborate windows at Snettisham and Cley along the coast. One hundred and forty angels hold up the hammerbeam roof at Knapton. Grotesque heads grin and leer from the lofty west front of the ruined Norman priory at Castle Acre. Perhaps the greatest of all the Norfolk churches is at Salle, north-west of Norwich. This great 15th-century building dominates the hamlet at its feet. The exterior, beautifully decorated, features feathered angels swinging censers and a pair of wild woodwoses brandishing clubs. The interior, high, magnificent and beautiful, is filled with clear light that pours in to light up the stonework and transport the worshipper.

Much of the Norfolk coast is for bird-watchers, walkers, yachtsmen and wild-fowlers. Such outdoor enthusiasts love the silence and space of the huge marshes that have grown through the slow and steady accumulation of silt, shingle and sand. There are sandy beaches, too, from bustling Great Yarmouth right round the curve of the coast to high-piled Cromer with its cosy Victorian atmosphere, old-fashioned pier (with a variety theatre at the end, just like Grandma used to love) and crumbling cliffs. Cromer crabs, caught by the town's inshore fishermen and prepared for the table by their wives, make an incomparably delicious dish when eaten on the day of capture. Further west stretches a string of

BELOW: The 140-mile (225-km) Viking Way runs southwards from the River Humber through Lincolnshire to reach Oakham in Rutland. Not far from the start of the path, walkers pass the isolated All Saints Church, standing alone on a spur of the Lincolnshire Wolds to the east of its parent village of Walesby.

ABOVE: The splendidly preserved windmill at Cley-next-the-Sea on the north Norfolk coast. A red brick tower mill complete with fantail, gallery and great white sails on 55-ft (17-m) crosspieces, it is dated 1713, but is probably largely a later rebuild. Corn was last ground here in 1917, and the mill was restored in 1961.

little coastal villages – Salthouse, Wiveton, Cley-next-the-Sea, Blakeney, Morston, Stiffkey. Once they throve on the coastal trade that came by ship to their salt water wharves. Now they stand a mile or more inland behind an apron of marshes that have smothered their sea trade. Muddy creeks connect some to the open sea, and here the boaters come to sail in safe water.

Round the corner by the resort of Hunstanton, and you are into Royal Norfolk, a tract of immaculately protected country around the royal holiday residence of Sandringham. Pine forests and heaths, sandy soil, pale ploughland, pretty villages... and one of the best bird-watching coasts in the country, facing west across the enormous flat wastes of the Wash Estuary. Here geese and ducks come in their millions from Siberia and other points far to the north, to over-winter among the mud flats, sandbanks and saltings. Seals breed here, too, and shellfish and invertebrates by the uncountable trillion. If you find a perch on the sea wall around Shepherd's Port, you can see 15 miles (24 kilometres) across the Wash to where lines of trees appear to be marching off out to sea – the dead flat coast of Lincolnshire.

With the help of binoculars you might even be able to make out Boston Stump, the giant tower of St Botolph's

Church which stands 272½ feet (83 metres) tall – that half-a-foot is insisted upon by every Bostonian worth his salt. It was from Boston in September 1607 that William Brewster and other pioneer puritan dissenters first tried to escape to the comparative religious liberty of the Low Countries. They were captured and brought back to Boston gaol in ignominy. The following year, though, they did get away to Holland. In 1620 these Pilgrim Fathers would pursue their dream of freedom to its conclusion, making the epic voyage to the New World aboard the *Mayflower*.

Boston was another of the east coast ports that declined as its sea lifeline silted up. The town also suffered from the competition of west coast ports like Liverpool and Bristol, so much more conveniently placed to receive goods from the colonies across the Atlantic – colonies, ironically, that William Brewster and his colleagues had helped to found. An 18th-century versifier pithily summed up Boston's plight back then:

Boston, Boston, thou hast naught to boast on,
But a Grand Sluice and a high steeple,
A proud, conceited, ignorant people,
And a coast where souls get lost on.

If you climb Boston Stump's 365 steps, you will be rewarded with a 100-mile (161-kilometre) round view. To all corners of the compass the earth looks dead flat. A great fertile plain of drained land stretches off into Norfolk in the south and east, runs up along a slanting coast of marsh and mud, and swings out north and west over Lincolnshire for 30 miles (48 kilometres) to the triple towers of the county's other great church, Lincoln Cathedral. This is a notable triumph of Norman architecture with its beautiful 13th-century rose window and angel roof. North-east of Lincoln rises the hump-backed range of the Lincolnshire Wolds, high country unexpectedly hilly for those who think of Lincolnshire as the flattest of counties. And north again stretches the wide, muddy barrier of the River Humber, where these East Anglian outposts stare across at Yorkshire and the North of England.

ABOVE RIGHT: Black sheep graze contentedly on the rich grass of the northern wolds of Lincolnshire. In medieval times the Lincolnshire Wolds were a vast sheepwalk, and the wool they produced brought tremendous prosperity to the local landowners.

RIGHT: Fishing boats hauled up on the beach at Cromer, north Norfolk.

# 7

# THE BROAD NORTH

CITIES, DALES, MOORS AND HILLS

ABOVE: Chester's famed
Rows, medieval shopping
lanes timbered in eye-
catching black-and-white.

OPPOSITE: Winter in the
Pennines: the scene near
Settle, North Yorkshire.

I GNORANT SOUTHERNERS will tell you that the North of England is all muck and money, smoke and slagheaps. This cartoon image is partly a hangover from the corrosive notion of the Great Divide, so deeply entrenched in Britain's national mythology, between the soft, effete south and the hard, practical north; partly it is founded on a reality that has long passed into history. It ignores the fact that the North's industrial areas, in spite of the powerful impression they make on an incomer, are very limited in extent compared with the enormous vistas of the rural northern landscape, its great wild moors, its green pastoral dales and dramatic coasts.

Coal, steel, steam and iron; textiles, shipbuilding, engineering; docks, mines, mills. They made the North the cradle and testbed of the Industrial Revolution; they made a few men as rich as Croesus, and enslaved millions of others; they fouled the rivers and defiled the landscape; they brought Britain untold wealth and influence, and underpinned the expansion of her empire. Between the 18th and 20th centuries the North of England was the undisputed champion of manufacture, proud to hold the title of 'Workshop of the World'.

Nowadays, around the turn of the third millennium, the North's heavy industry is a dinosaur long dead and buried. The great cities and grimy towns founded on trade and industry have passed through a profound late-20th-century depression. They are beginning to find themselves new roles as conference venues, centres of modern technology, leisure zones – even as tourist destinations, exploiting their vast industrial heritage. The twin cities of Liverpool and Manchester – neighbours and rivals – give a vivid snapshot of the past glories and future aspirations of such mercantile and manufacturing giants. The dock basins, warehouses and grandiose harbour offices of once-mighty Liverpool, founded on transatlantic trade as exotic as rum and pineapples and as sad as slaves and destitute emigrants, are now refurbished as museums, galleries, restaurants, pleasant promenades. Manchester's cavernous textile ware-houses and cotton-trading halls are hives of boutiques, theatres, apartments, cafés; her urban waterways are lined with gay bars and fashionable night-spots; its ship canal quays have sprouted a forest of architects' offices, theme pubs and desirable executive homes. There are still wide tracts of disused industrial plant and of grim housing estates fit for demolition, but cities like these no longer look with despair on the legacy they inherited from the Industrial Revolution. There is a buzz and an optimism about them, a new energy that attracts youngsters.

The solidity and confidence of great industrial architecture, the pride that saw city-centre warehouses embellished with terracotta floral mouldings – these are easy to admire. But what of the belts of industrial dereliction that surround many of the northern ex-manufacturing cities – spoil heaps, pithead yards, steel mills, quarry

holes? These are still plain to see in the post-industrial landscape. Some have already been found new rôles as games fields, lakes or landscaped suburban parks. But ought they to be smoothed away entirely, expunged so thoroughly that future generations will be unable to read their own histories and trace their roots in these stark places?

If the industrial past is beginning to fade in the consciousness of young northerners, the age-old rivalry between Lancashire and Yorkshire runs as strongly – if not quite as bloodily – as it did when the ducal houses of these two adjacent counties clashed over the succession to the throne of England during the Wars of the Roses more than 500 years ago. Yorkshire, the White Rose county, boasts the greatness of its cricketers; Lancashire of the Red Rose points to the footballers of Manchester United. Yorkshire's fortunes were founded on wool; Lancashire looked to King Cotton for prosperity. Yorkshire's factory workers flocked to Scarborough's sands for their holidays; Lancashire's millhands crowded out Blackpool ('noted for fresh air and fun') during their precious weeks off. Blackpool in particular still fulfils every requirement of the archetypal British seaside holiday – crowded sands, variety shows, the Golden Mile of flashy amusement arcades and chip shops, the glitz and white-knuckle thrills of the funfair, as well as slot-machines and strolling on the pier.

A few miles north of Manchester the Lancashire valley of Rossendale slides east across the border to become Calderdale in Yorkshire. Here stand the cotton and wool towns where it all began: Haslingden, Rawtenstall and Bacup, Todmorden and Hebden Bridge, huddled places of gritstone with the east Lancashire and west Yorkshire moors rising at their backs. Fifty years ago this string of towns along its tight valley-floor corridor of road, railway, river and canal lay under a thick pall of domestic and industrial coal smoke. The buildings were crusted black with soot and oxidisation, adding to the grimness of the scene under the dark moors. Every cobbled valley-bottom street echoed with the roar and rattle of textile machinery from the big mills. Now, with their gritstone cleaned to a sparkling creaminess, the thunder of their looms stilled for ever, the towns have a quiet, intimate beauty. Cobbled packhorse trails lead over humpbacked bridges and up across the moors,

ABOVE: Wool wealth enriched the landowners and mill masters of the West Riding of Yorkshire, but the handloom weavers led a hard and underpaid working life.

RIGHT: A canalside scene at Hebden Bridge in the West Riding of Yorkshire. As the Industrial Revolution gathered pace at the end of the 18th century, spawning canal transport and then steam power, the factories moved down from their original hillside locations beside the streams that had powered their machinery. They settled in long lines along the valley floors of Lancashire and Yorkshire where the roads and canals, and later the railways, all ran.

through a scatter of bleak Methodist chapels and short terraces of cottages with long, many-mullioned windows. Crawshawbooth, Goodshaw, Heptonstall, Wadsworth – these were the settlements of the original 18th-century weavers at the start of the Industrial Revolution. John Wesley, William Darney and the other great pioneers of Nonconformist religion knew these moor-edge villages well, riding and walking to isolated farms and barns full of clandestine worshippers who risked mockery, beatings and sometimes worse if discovered.

A little further north across the broad, rolling shoulders of the Calderdale moors lies Brontë country, the windswept moorlands around the west Yorkshire village of Haworth where the Reverend Patrick Brontë brought up his son and three daughters in the old Parsonage. The son, poor Branwell Brontë, died young and raddled with drink and self-dislike; but the three sisters were to give English literature one of its most spectacular brief flowerings during the 1840s. During the *annus mirabilis* of 1847, Charlotte (1816–1855) published *Jane Eyre*, Anne (1820–1849) produced *The Tenant of Wildfell Hall*; while Emily (1818–1848) brought out her masterpiece and only novel, *Wuthering Heights*, set in the harsh moorlands around her village and centred on the remote farmhouse of Top Withens. Emily was to die the following year from the family curse of consumption, or tuberculosis. She fiercely loved these moors where her

ABOVE: The ruins of Top Withens, the farmhouse on the sombre West Yorkshire moors that inspired Emily Brontë to create *Wuthering Heights*.

ABOVE: Deep, dark and lonely: Wastwater in the western Lake District.

OPPOSITE: Hillwalkers stretch their legs and get away from it all on a strenuous hike across Martindale Common, high above Ullswater in the north-east corner of the Lake District.

wild spirit could roam day and night, free of her sick body, as one of her most passionate poems declares:

High waving heather, 'neath stormy blasts bending,
Midnight and moonlight and bright shining stars;
Darkness and glory rejoicingly blending,
Earth rising to heaven and heaven descending,
Man's spirit away from its drear dungeon sending,
Bursting the fetters and breaking the bars.

From the Brontë moors the Pennine Hills, the high spine of the North of England, undulate north into limestone country starred with bright flowers. The dales are rich grazing country, and the higher moors give splendid walking on fractured limestone pavement or long grassy slopes, with vast views under even vaster skies. This is lonely sheep-farming country, skirting the wide, empty uplands of the Forest of Bowland before striding further north towards Hadrian's Wall and the Scottish border.

North-west of Bowland, tightly folded into a circle of lakes and mountains, lies the Lake District, jewel of the North. In these 900 square miles (2,331 square kilometres) the four single elements of water, woodland, hills and sky blend with subtle magic, so that a scene you think you know well can change the nature of its allure completely between one cloud shadow and the next. The Lake District has none of the craggy hauteur of the Alps: its peaks are not really peaks at all, but

rounded brows. They inspire delight, and even awe, but they are not overawing. Coming here with a decent pair of walking boots, even those who have never climbed a mountain feel that they can tackle Helvellyn, Scafell Pike, Haystacks, Great Gable and the other splendid heights of the region. That is really the magic of the Lake District: you respect the landscape, and you love it too, intimately and warmly. Yet it constantly surprises you, with a shift of light or a meteoric change of mood.

In these parts, steep slopes of ground are known as fells (a fell is a little more than a hill, and rather less than a mountain). There are nearly 200 Lake District fells that top 2,000 feet (610 metres), but only four attain the 3,000-foot (914-metre) mark – an indication of the steep but unthreatening nature of the terrain. Lakes and reservoirs, most of them long and narrow, form the curved spokes of the Lake District wheel between the fell ranges, and the whole thing centres – most appropriately – on the village and lake of Grasmere at the heart of the district.

It is impossible to write of the Lake District without thinking of William Wordsworth (1770–1850), the heart and soul of Lakeland poetry. The *Journal* kept by his sister Dorothy (1771–1855) of their life together at the turn of the 19th century in Dove Cottage at Grasmere, beautifully observed and written, was the touchstone and inspiration of so many of William's poems. Before Wordsworth's time, landscape as rugged and little-frequented as the Lakeland fells was thought of as barbarous and frightening: 'A country,' wrote Daniel Defoe in the 1720s, 'eminent only for being the wildest, most barren and frightful of any that I have passed over.' It took painters like Thomas Gainsborough (1727–1788), John Constable (1776–1837) and J. M. W. Turner (1775–1851), and poets such as Thomas Gray, Robert Southey (1774–1843) and, of course, Wordsworth himself, to spread the idea that the Lake District was in fact sublimely beautiful.

The main fells and lakes at the centre of the area are the chief attraction. By contrast, the country that encircles them – much of it coastal, most of it fascinating – plays a very muted second fiddle. Yet here are vast tidal sands in the south (well over 100 square miles [259 square kilometres] exposed at low tides) thrust into by three thick green fingers of peninsulas. Here stand the impressive ruins of Cartmel Priory and Furness Abbey. One of the strangest and most exciting walks in Britain is the crossing of the sands of Morecambe Bay in the wake of the official Sands Guide. Three rivers come down to the sea through the sands – the Kent, the Keer and the Leven – and the Kent in particular can change its course from one day to the next. Only the Guide knows just how river,

Further north up the Cumbrian coast are superb red sandstone cliffs around bays of warm silvery-black sand, fishing villages, and long stretches of quiet farmland. This is an area with a severely depressed economy: only the nuclear reprocessing plant at Sellafield has offered much in the way of employment since the coal mines closed down and inshore fishing went into decline a generation ago. Whitehaven, halfway up the

coast, was built as a planned town during the 17th century by the immensely rich and influential coal-owning Lowther family, and enhanced with some very fine public buildings – Assembly Rooms, public baths, churches – and plenty of grand merchants' houses during its Georgian heyday. By the 1970s, though, the coal pits were closed, the houses rotting and the public buildings decaying. Whitehaven was a sad slump town, out on a limb, forgotten. Then a huge renovation project got under way, supported by big cash injections from the town's main employer, British Nuclear Fuels. Many of the derelict old Georgian houses have been renovated, the public buildings put back on their feet, the shabby dockside areas cleaned up. The dignified appearance of a handsome old seaport town, having almost faded away like a poor-quality photographic print, is shaping itself and strengthening again.

Back to the Pennine Chain, that smoothly swollen, irregularly humped backbone of Britain. If you want to get a feeling for the real wildness of the North, and an insight into both west and east sides of the region, take to the 250-mile (402-kilometre) Pennine Way National Trail that runs the whole length of the chain. It's a hell of a three-week slog, with enough leg-sucking

ABOVE: Lake District waterfalls are known as 'ghylls', a good Norse word.

ABOVE RIGHT: Whitehaven was built during the 17th and 18th centuries by the Lowther family, local coal-mine owners. After the mines closed during the 20th century, Whitehaven slumped into decay. But recent injections of cash have seen much of the handsome Georgian town restored.

tide and sand are juxtaposed from one day to the next. He stakes his course out by placing laurel sprigs called 'brobs' along the route, and woe betide those who stray – an unpleasant death by drowning or quicksand awaits them. It is an unbeatable thrill to make the three- or four-hour crossing with the Guide, splashing through the rivers up to one's knees, watching flocks of wading birds grow until they fill the lower sky, and seeing the tide collect itself on the southern horizon in preparation for its charge in across the bay. You do all this in the full knowledge that within an hour or so the firm sands under your feet will be sucking quicksands, and the sea will be flowing 20 feet (6 metres) above the place where you are walking.

peat bog and rain-lashed moorland to reduce even the toughest to tears. Yet the impression that remains, long after the blisters have healed and the thigh muscles ceased to twang, is of glorious freedom in wind, rain and sun, and of the great variety of scenery it marches you through – in particular in Yorkshire, through which its central, some would say its best, section runs.

'Best bloody country in Britain – or anywhere else, come to that,' Yorkshiremen will tell you, with all the shrinking diffidence of a heavyweight boxing champion at a weigh-in. They have a point. Yorkshire is by far the biggest county in England, and its landscapes are as varied as they are striking. The county, not content with having two entire national parks to itself – the

Yorkshire Dales and the North York Moors – appropriates in its southernmost reaches the tip of the Peak National Park.

The Dales, lush river valleys under harsh moor tops, cut down through the peat and limestone of the upland Pennines. Their beauty is the beauty of contrast between valley floors and lower sides tailored through the centuries for agriculture, with walls, barns and farmhouses all built of the pale grey stone, and the uplands above the intake walls where it is moorland grazing and peat bogs, the scars of mineral mining and endless miles of supreme walking country.

Nidderdale, Wharfedale and Ribblesdale run from north to south with a touch of east; Wensleydale and

ABOVE: The Yorkshire Dales National Park contains some of the most varied and beautiful scenery in Britain – rugged moors, hill ranges, glorious green dales striped with miles of drystone walls, wooded river valleys and snug little stone-built villages. No wonder it is one of the most popular areas for car-borne sightseeing; also for walking, with its magnificent network of footpaths.

ABOVE: This superb view
across Dentdale is the reward
for climbing Whernside. Tough
and determined hikers can
try tackling the 24-mile
(39-km) Three Peaks
Challenge, which involves
climbing three fells –
Whernside (2,416 ft [736 m]),
Ingleborough (2,376 ft
[723 m]) and Pen-y-ghent
(2,231 ft [694 m]) – in no
more than 12 hours.

Swaledale flow from west to east. Wensleydale is the
broadest and most pastoral, famous for its grazing and
its cheese, and for the scenic attraction of Aysgarth
Falls. Swaledale to the north is a harsher proposition:
here the farmers in the tiny villages of Muker, Keld and
Gunnerside, high up the dale, cling on to their liveli-
hoods with ever-slackening grip as public services
wither away and townies from Leeds and Bradford buy
up the pretty houses. The Pennine Way passes
through, bringing a little bed-and-breakfast trade from
tired and muddy walkers only too ready to relax and
appreciate the beauty of the dale. (Landladies who
offer an evening meal – especially if it features that
incomparable Yorkshire treat for the tastebuds, a crisp
home-made Yorkshire pudding – get extra plus points
from Pennine Way pilgrims.) Keeping agriculture

going in its long-established patterns – hay-cutting,
wall-mending, wintering animals on the valley floors
and summering higher up, shearing and selling, milking
and foddering – is the only way to maintain the ordered
beauty of this or any other dale; a way of life sadly at
odds with modern farming and economic practice.

Nidderdale towards the east of the Pennines has its
string of reservoirs winking like eyes. Ribblesdale on the
west boasts moors as wild and lonely as any in the North,
and is bestridden by the 24 arches of the Ribblehead
Viaduct. This astonishing masterpiece of Victorian
railway architecture carries Britain's most dramatically
lonely railway line, the 72-mile (116-kilometre) Settle &
Carlisle Railway. It is Wharfedale in the centre of the
region, however, that can claim to be the heart of the
Dales. The River Wharfe in its limestone bed of rocky

cups and hollows rushes down narrow Langstrothdale, a northern extension of Wharfedale proper, below farmhouses built Viking-style all of a piece with their barns and carrying Viking names: Oughtershaw, Beckermonds, Yockenthwaite, Hubberholme. At Hubberholme ('the flat land by the river where Hubba lives') there is a little riverside church with a Tudor rood loft dated 1558 – it must have been made in the very last days of the reign of the fanatically Roman Catholic Queen Mary. The wooden mice carved into the pews are the sign and symbol of noted 20th-century woodcarver Robert Thompson. Beyond the bridge stands the ancient George Inn, where a local field known as the Poor Field is auctioned for rent each New Year. A candle on the bar is lit; the last bid to be offered before it gutters out is the one accepted, and the money goes to charity.

Further down dale is a string of picturesque villages – Buckden, Starbotton, Kettlewell, Grassington – before the Wharfe plunges into the glorious oak and beech woods of Bolton Abbey. The river has a furious and spectacular tussle to force its way through The Strid, a constricted channel of rock almost narrow enough to jump across – almost, but not quite, as many have found to their cost. Downstream, in calmer water, the Wharfe flows in a graceful bend under the much painted and photographed ruins of Bolton Abbey, a Norman priory church in a most beautiful situation of meadows, woods and river.

If the Yorkshire Dales National Park shows a gentler side to the county, the North York Moors are closer to the stereotypical image of Yorkshire folk: hard, blunt, unforgiving, dour, but with a heart of gold. On first acquaintance these endlessly rolling, dark-hued uplands, in parts patched with sombre conifer forests, can look forbidding, even menacing. But they are wonderfully rewarding to explore, especially on foot. The Cleveland Way long distance footpath skirts their western and northern boundaries before passing down their easterly coastal rim; the infamously mucky Lyke Wake Walk route crosses them. There are numerous other, shorter paths; one of the best is a 12-mile (19-kilometre) circuit that connects beautiful Rosedale with pretty little Hutton-le-Hole and the reconstructed

Little fishing and former iron-working villages are tucked into hollows at the feet of the cliffs. Staithes is a charming place, living on tourism more than fishing these days and happy to exploit its connection with the young James Cook (1728–1779). The embryo explorer was born at Marton a few miles west, and acted as shop boy to a Staithes grocer until maltreatment or a thirst for adventure induced him to pocket a shilling from the shop till and run away to Whitby just down the coast.

Whitby, too, delights in its Captain Cook associations; the young man served a ship-building apprenticeship in

ABOVE: The 24 arches of the Ribblehead Viaduct, opened in 1875, carry the Settle & Carlisle Railway across a bleak and boggy moor.

historic buildings at the Ryedale Folk Museum. Another grand and less effortful way to look into the heart of the moor is to ride the steam trains of the North York Moors Railway, a slow, 18-mile (29-kilometre) chug between Pickering on the National Park's southern border and Grosmont near the northern edge. From Newtondale Halt there is a gorgeous walk to view the great water-scooped Hole of Horcum; from Goathland Station under Wheeldale Moor (haunt of many a witch), a long flight of steps leads down to the beautiful waterfall of Mallyan Spout, a 70 foot (20-metre) chute of water down a mossy rock face in a cleft of the moor.

The Yorkshire coast runs south for 90 miles (145 kilometres) from Staithes to Spurn Head. All the drama and spectacle are in the more northerly half, the 'Captain Cook coast' of tall cliffs that were much mined in times past for alum, jet, iron and other minerals.

the town, and insisted on Whitby-built vessels (including both his famous ships, *Resolution* and *Endeavour*) for his voyages of exploration into the South Seas and around Australia. Cook's apprentice-master, John Walker, lived in Grape Lane, and his house is now a very striking and well administered memorial museum to Captain Cook. But Whitby is not entirely given over to 'Cookitis'. There is a fine Norman parish church, full of ship-wright-made Georgian woodwork and high box pews, perched on the cliffs at the top of the 199 Church Stairs. In its graveyard Bram Stoker (1847–1912) had Count Dracula, transformed into a hellish hound after surviving the wreck of the *Demeter*, seek shelter in a suicide's grave. Beyond soar the delicate medieval stone arches and columns of Whitby Abbey in their clifftop location. Hereabouts stood the Saxon abbey (destroyed by Danish marauders in AD 867), where in

664 the epoch-making Synod of Whitby decided on a nation-wide adoption of Roman Catholic rather than Celtic rites of worship, along with Rome's system of centralised organisation.

Further on down the coast, camera-friendly Robin Hood's Bay huddles into its cliffs, a charming vista of red patched roofs at crazy angles spilling down roadways too steep and narrow to admit a car. Then comes brash and cheerful Scarborough, with its two fine beaches separated by a long jut of headland crowned with impressive castle ruins. A dignified old spa town with its handsome clifftop esplanades, its terraces and public buildings, Scarborough became a good-time resort for Yorkshire's Victorian working classes. Elements of both characters cling to the town, one of the few English seaside resorts still to be doing good holiday business.

ABOVE: Low tide in Runswick Bay, North Yorkshire. The bait-diggers extract lugworm and ragworm to use as bait for their sea-angling tackle. The result is a fine haul of cod.

RIGHT: Puffing through the moors: the North York Moors Railway, a beautifully preserved steam railway reopened in 1973 along the 18-mile (29-km) line.

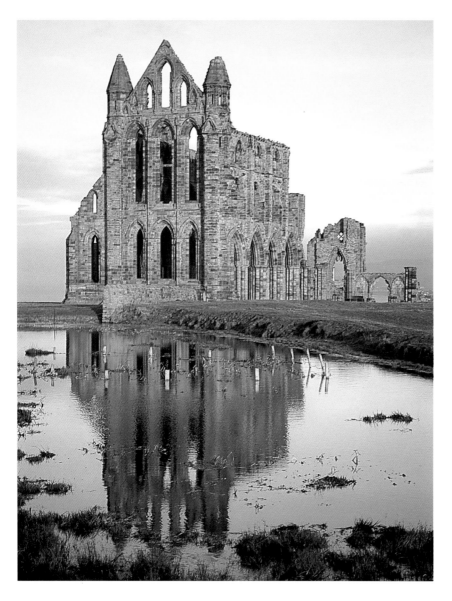

The high cliffs continue south as far as the bulbous, cave-burrowed headland of Flamborough Head. From here they decline into Holderness, the southern half of the Yorkshire coast that maintains an almost imperceptible south-eastward curve for nearly 50 miles (80 kilometres). The low cliffs of soft, dark clay are being eaten by the North Sea at a frightening speed. Each winter's storms bite another 10 feet (3 metres) inland, causing houses, sheds and caravans to topple to destruction on the sands below. From the southernmost end curves the 3-mile-long (5-kilometre-long) Spurn Peninsula, a languidly bent finger only 100 yards (91 metres) wide. At its seaward end stand two lighthouses – a salt-stained redundant light, and a more modern and still operative one. Here, too, lives a small community of lifeboatmen, the only permanently maintained and paid professional crew in Britain, a bulwark in the defence of seafarers' lives in the treacherous waters around Spurn. Henry Bolingbroke landed here from the Continent in 1399, on his way to depose King Richard II and seize the throne of England. The spit is regularly breached by storms, and as regularly repaired. But now the thinking is to leave it be, to let the sea have it as the natural end result of a natural process. In time it will recreate itself a little further into the Humber Estuary: former Spurns have done so at 250-year intervals down the millennia. Their ghost shapes lie out under the North Sea in parallel ranks like spoons curved in a cutlery canteen, along with the ghost streets of Monkwike and Monkwell, Southorpe and Northorpe – former villages of Holderness, long ago swallowed by the sea.

Inland from Holderness sits York, capital city of Yorkshire and one of Britain's most beautiful and

ABOVE: Seafarers' landmark, *Dracula* fans' icon: the clifftop ruins of Whitby Abbey. The abbey was founded in AD 657, destroyed by the Danes in 867, and refounded in 1078; what stands today is mostly Early English work that dates from around 1220.

RIGHT: The sea-bitten cliffs and caves of Flamborough Head, a chalk promontory on the Yorkshire coast, where ferocious tides and currents have brought many ships to grief.

historic cities. York's appeal has much to do with the almost intact state of its 13th-century city walls, a diamond-shaped belt of pale limestone 2½ miles (4 kilometres) in circumference that both constricts and preserves the medieval heart of the city. Four great bars or gates pierce the walls – Monk Bar, Walmgate Bar, Micklegate Bar and Bootham Bar – their turrets and arrow slits frowning down on traffic passing under their low archways. You can stroll a circuit of York's walls along a raised walkway inside the parapet, looking down across the city's narrow medieval streets or 'gates' (in York a bar is a gate, and a gate is a street). Gillygate, Fossgate, Goodramgate; Stonegate, Deangate, Whip-ma-whop-ma-gate – evocative names all. York's gates are overhung with old houses, some dating back to pre-Tudor times. A clutch of excellent museums explains the city's rich history, from its establishment as the Roman garrison town of Eboracum, through Saxon

pre-eminence as a centre of learning and a Viking incarnation as Jorvik, and on through medieval wool wealth and Georgian popularity as a fashionable inland resort.

Chief glory of York is the splendid cathedral church known as York Minster, which sails like a giant ship inside the northern apex of the walls. Only the Archbishop of Canterbury outranks the Archbishop of York in the Church of England's ecclesiastical hierarchy, and many think York Minster the finest cathedral in Britain. It is northern Europe's largest ancient church, an astonishing achievement by architects and masons with only medieval technology to help them. The original Norman church still lives partially on in ground plan in the crypt, but the Minster as it stands was begun in 1220. It took two-and-a-half centuries to finish this mighty building, with its many-pinnacled twin west towers and its square-topped central tower. There is a superb octagonal late-13th-century chapter

ABOVE: Pioneer South Seas explorer James Cook served as a ship-building apprentice in Whitby.

house, richly carved with humans, beasts, birds and foliage sprays. The nave climbs impressively to 100 feet (30 metres). But the treasure of the Minster is its wonderful medieval stained glass: 13th-century grisaille, or grey glass, in the tall lancets of the Five Sisters window in the north transept, even older glass in the clerestory windows, 14th-century glass filling the west window, which soars 54 feet (15 metres) high. There is glowing red and blue Tudor glass in the south transept's rose window. It was installed to commemorate the 1486 marriage between Henry Tudor of the House of Lancaster and Princess Elizabeth of York, a union which effectively drew a firm line under the 30 years of bitter civil strife that we call the Wars of the Roses.

ABOVE: Medieval walls continue to surround York city and provide a memorial to their skilled craftsmen.

The stonework of York Minster soars and arches with slender grace. Across the border in County Durham the architecture of Durham Cathedral, York's only serious rival in the North of England, stands solid, dogged and foursquare, a reflection of the mailed-fist power of the Norman dynasty under which it was built. By the time work was beginning on the great medieval phase of York Minster, Durham Cathedral was all but complete. It is a huge building, the impression of grim power made all the more striking by its position jutting over the River Wear from a slim high-backed peninsula at the heart of Durham City. Just across Palace Green stands Durham Castle. The two great buildings, side by side on their eminence, trumpet the power, consequence and enormous wealth of the medieval Prince Bishops of Durham who lived in the one and worshipped in the other. The Prince

Bishops, given a virtually free hand by the English monarch in the eternal fight against their turbulent neighbours and enemies the Scots, ruled like kings themselves from this peninsular fortress. Their cathedral, built of pale rose-coloured stone, has splendid squat cylindrical pillars marching off down the nave, carved with patterns of dogtooth, chevron and lozenge. They stand in striking contrast to the slender, almost delicate pillars and vaulting of the Galilee Chapel at the west end of the cathedral, where St Cuthbert's biographer the Venerable Bede [673–735] is buried, and the Chapel of the Nine Altars at the east end where Cuthbert himself, the shepherd saint and bishop, lies under a plain marble slab.

In the cathedral's treasury is kept the pectoral cross of St Cuthbert, along with the warped old timbers of his wooden coffin, carved with round-eyed Byzantine depictions of the apostles. These precious relics were taken from the saint's tomb during one of several openings and inspections over the centuries. It was said that Cuthbert's body remained miraculously uncorrupted after his death in AD 687; and the saint's resting place has been disturbed several times by inquisitive believers, as well as by iconoclastic zealots at the time of the Reformation. Cuthbert himself, a wise and wonderfully skilled orator, was reluctantly persuaded to quit his preferred solitude on the sea-battered Farne Islands off the Northumbrian coast in order to give a spiritual lead to the Christians in the North. He would have preferred to have been left alone with the seals and seabirds, but the world needed him too much to let him be. After his death, too, his body was shifted around from one place to another for more than 100 years to prevent it falling into the hands of the Vikings, until a vision indicated to his faithful followers (and bearers) that he should be laid to rest at Dun Holme, the place of the Dun Cow – Durham.

Durham City is a compact place, ideal for strolling the twisting streets, cobbled laneways and paths beside the River Wear. The countryside around the city still carries the scars of the now-defunct Durham coal mining industry, once so profitable and so dominant in the country. To the east is an all-but-unvisited coast. Some of its beaches are fouled with old mine waste, but others are clean and beautiful. A fine run of cliffs is indented by green, thickly wooded clefts, known here as 'denes', where bird-watchers in the know can spot rarities migrated or blown in from the North Sea.

Out to the west of Durham City the land steepens into the beautiful wild moorland of Weardale and Teesdale, eastern Pennine country where narrow moor roads wriggle over the fells and the windswept high

commons above little country towns such as Stanhope, Barnard Castle and Middleton-in-Teesdale. In spring the upper reaches of Teesdale are jewelled with royal blue spring gentians, Teesdale violets, blush-pink birds-eye primroses and other extremely rare survivals of the arctic-alpine flora that thrived in Britain after the last Ice Age. And here the dolerite shelf known as the Whin Sill outcrops in the spectacular 100-foot (30-metre) staircase of High Force, down which after rainfall the Tees leaps and thunders in violent cascade.

And so to England's northernmost county, the least densely populated and, some would say, the most bleakly beautiful of the lot – Northumberland. Not that you would guess at the lonely character of the county from the point at which most people enter, the vibrantly lively city of Newcastle-upon-Tyne, home of the darkly humorous Geordies. Shipbuilding along the River Tyne and coal-mining in the country round about, the traditional industries, are dead and gone. But with typical resilience Newcastle has reinvented itself as the shopping and night-life mecca of the North-East, the place to go if you want a reasonably rowdy good time.

Up beyond the city, though, the essential loneliness, harsh beauty and melancholy of the Northumbrian

ABOVE: The impressive ruins of a Norman fortress stand high above the River Tees at Barnard Castle. The castle was founded in 1125–40, and extended and strengthened during the 13th century.

RIGHT: Kittiwakes on Inner Farne: the lonely islands are a haven for seabirds. The shepherd saint Cuthbert so appreciated their remoteness that he holed up on Inner Farne for eight years (AD 676–684), and returned there after two years as Bishop of Lindisfarne, to die on 20 March 687 in the peace and isolation he craved.

ABOVE: Winter in the Cheviot
Hills, when a dusting of snow
brings out all the bleak
grandeur of this range of
grassy, bog-strewn hills along
the Scottish border. Their wild
beauty is best depicted in the
haunting music of the
Northumbrian smallpipes.

landscape quickly asserts itself. Three great old roads ribbon away for the Scottish Border and Edinburgh: through Otterburn to Jedburgh, through Wooler to Coldstream, through Berwick-on-Tweed to the East Lothian coast. The former two encompass Northumberland's defining range of hills, the windy peat-bog heights of Cheviot. The Cheviot Hills slant north-east, with the Scottish border running along their spine. Rounded hills clothed in short grass and heather, they do not touch 3,000 feet (914 metres). But they are so remote and under-populated, so little frequented even by long-distance walkers, that they take on a character of true wildness. A good road to take if you want to get an authentic taste of Cheviot and of inner Northumberland is the one that shadows the River Coquet through Rothbury and on by way of Thropton, Hepple, Sharperton and Harbottle, to Alwinton in the throat of Upper Coquetdale. These are sheep-farming places, where stark old defensive blockhouses known as pele towers poke up among the trees. Hereabouts the

winter snows, the sheep sales and the annual Rothbury gathering of Northumbrian pipers are still the touchstones of the calendar. Up in Upper Coquetdale the road winds past Shillmoor, Windyhaugh, Blindburn and Bleakhope, evocative names for back-of-beyond farms under great shoulders of grassy fells. You can climb to the border from these farms by way of Clennell Street, Salter's Road, Dere Street or Gamel's Path, ancient trade and drove tracks across the lonely hills. Conifers choke the deep-sided valleys. Burns crash down their shallow, stony beds. The wind is ever-present. Up at Windy Gyle, splashing along the bleakest section of the Pennine Way, you tread in the footsteps of cattle thieves, salt traders, soldiers and outlaws. Proud local lairdlings and their followers hacked each other to pieces with abandon all over this countryside, before the Union of England and Scotland in 1707 brought a breath of outside law and a measure of stability to the lawless Borders.

The Romans would have given short shrift to such anarchic behaviour. In fact it was to suppress any like

tendencies that in AD 120 Emperor Hadrian ordered the building of a wall clean across the neck of the country from the North Sea at Wallsend in the east to the Solway Firth in the west. It was at one and the same time a solid defensive barrier against the barbarians of Caledonia, a statement that the Romans were in Britain to stay, and a physical full stop to the northern limits of the Roman Empire. Hadrian's Wall was built of carefully shaped and fitted stone blocks. It stood 15 feet (5 metres) tall, rising to 21 feet (6 metres) at the crest of its battlements. It was 8 feet (2 metres) thick, with a garrisoned castle at each milepost and a major fort every 5 miles (8 kilometres).

Hadrian's Wall was a stark piece of work, manned by provincial conscripts from outposts of the Empire, often shrouded in mist, usually cold and rainy. Not the Roman army's most popular posting, one might guess. But it operated effectively for almost 300 years, and is still traceable with remarkable clarity in the landscape as deep ditches, foundation plans of forts and many

long stretches of the Wall itself. Stones from the Wall, fragments of carved inscriptions from Roman tombstones, pagan altar stones and roadway paving have been collected in museums the length of the Wall. They also live on in the walls of local barns, churches and farmhouses, harvested down the centuries by prudent Northumbrians from what they clearly regarded as a huge, providential linear dump of ready-made building materials.

Out to the east runs the Northumberland coast, 70 miles (113 kilometres) of the chilliest, windiest and most blissfully uncrowded sand and pebble beaches in England. Dramatic ruined castles frown from the cliffs: Dunstanburgh and Bamburgh. If the weather and the sea were 10 degrees warmer, the Northumbrian coast would be the playground of millions. Thank goodness they are not. Here you can walk for miles on clean sand, and see no one.

Low-lying islands ride the storms a mile or so offshore. Coquet Island, off the old coal port of Amble, is

ABOVE: Hadrian's Wall has ridden the dolerite wave of the Whin Sill since Emperor Hadrian ordered its construction in AD 120 to keep the Caledonian barbarians out of this northernmost outpost of the Roman Empire. The shaped stone blocks of the 73-mile (117-km) Wall and its lookout towers and garrison buildings were 'quarried' for local buildings over the ensuing two millennia. Nowadays, it is restored and provided with an accompanying long-distance National Trail footpath.

a sanctuary for puffins and terns. Further north the long dark outlines of the Farne Islands, outposts of the dolerite Whin Sill, break the North Sea like a fleet of surfacing submarines. At high tide there are 15, at low tide 28. They form little tribal families: the Wideopens, the Harcars, the Wamses. It was on Big Harcar that the paddle-steamer *Forfarshire* ran aground in September 1838. From his lighthouse on Longstone, the most sea-ward of the Farnes, Keeper Darling and his daughter Grace set out in their little boat to snatch the survivors of the wreck from the rock – one of the most famous sea rescue stories of all time. And it was on Inner Farne, haunted by goat-riding demons, that St Cuthbert spent eight years as a solitary hermit, wrestling with himself, God and the Devil, until in AD 684 he was begged and coerced away to become Bishop of the holy island of Lindisfarne and a reluctant participant in mainland life and politics. The saint did manage to end his life as he had wished, however, returning to see out his last days on Inner Farne, where he died on 20 March 687.

Lindisfarne or Holy Island lies just up the coast, a leg-of-mutton-shaped island reached via a muddy causeway only uncovered for a few hours each tide. There is a small, wind-bitten grey stone village, a grim castle on a crag, acres of sand dunes, acres of mud and sand flats – and the tremendous and inspiring ruins of a great Benedictine church and priory. It was built at the outset of the 12th century by monks faithful to the outpost spirit that had caught and maintained the light of Christianity on Lindisfarne all through the Dark Ages when it had wavered and expired on the northern mainland. St Cuthbert was Prior of that first precarious monastic community on Holy Island, though he soon removed himself to the Farnes for greater isolation. Immediately following his death, Cuthbert's comrade monks of the Lindisfarne commu-nity created one of the most beautiful books on earth, the sublimely illustrated Lindisfarne Gospels. The book has somehow survived the vicissitudes of 1,300 years, and rests in the British Museum. Legend says that it fell into the sea while being ferried to safety, and sank out of sight. But the following morning it was found on the beach, washed ashore without a single stain or blur.

North of Holy Island stands Berwick, ancient border town on the River Tweed. Berwick is on the English side of the border – for the present. The town changed hands between English and Scots no fewer than 13 times between 1147 and 1482, usually accompanied by rape, pillage and butchery. Such were the forthright politics of the medieval border. As for the future ... who can say?

OPPOSITE: View across the sands to Holy Island, with Lindisfarne Castle perched on the rocky outcrop of Beblowe Crag.

ABOVE: The windswept, haunting beauty of the Farne Islands, where St Cuthbert lived as a hermit from 676–684.

BELOW: Thousands of puffins burrow their nesting holes into the sparse turf of Northumberland's offshore islands, making the surface as fragile as tissue paper in hot dry summers.

# 8

# THE LOWLANDS
# OF SCOTLAND

## FROM THE LONELY BORDER HILLS
## TO THE BEAUTIES OF THE TROSSACHS

ABOVE: In medieval conflicts between England and Scotland, the Border town of Berwick-upon-Tweed changed hands thirteen times.

OPPOSITE: The Douglas clan's stronghold of Tantallon Castle frowns across to where the gannet-haunted basalt plug of the Bass Rock rises from the waters of the Firth of Forth.

SCOTLAND IS ANOTHER COUNTRY: they do things differently there. Not as differently as some Scots would like to claim, but far more differently than many Englishmen fondly imagine. You sense the change almost as soon as you cross the border. Views are wider, the earth and rocks redden, pubs look less cosy, towns neater. Bleak defensive towers and castle ruins stand on knolls and cliff edges, proclaiming the Scottish Borders a land with a bloody past. So it was – fought over, won and lost, taken and relinquished again and again by both nations; soaked in blood, too, by the constant feuding in medieval times between the local families: Maxwells, Johnstones, Crichtons, Armstrongs, Douglases. Cattle-raiding, mutual house-burning and the making and breaking of alliances were a way of life, celebrated (and romanticised) by Sir Walter Scott (1771–1832) in his 1802/3 'Border ballads', and not finally expunged until long after the Act of Union that joined Scotland and England in 1707.

Some of that old, rugged history comes to light along the Berwickshire and East Lothian coast that runs north from Berwick-on-Tweed. There are grim walls on the clifftops near St Abb's Head – the ruins of Fast Castle, which Sir Walter Scott used as the template for Wolf's Crag in *The Bride of Lammermoor*, the 'solitary and naked tower, situated on a projecting cliff that beetled on the German Ocean'. Even grimmer and more dour is the mighty fortress of Tantallon Castle near North Berwick, a sandstone stronghold of the Douglas clan, whose walls plunge sheer to sea cliffs. But this south-eastern coast of Scotland is more about fishing than fighting these days; small-scale inshore fishing for crabs from tiny harbours such as Burnmouth, or bigger trawler fleets based on towns like Eyemouth and Dunbar. The sea has carved the cliffs into jagged headlands and coves, and is an implacable enemy as well as a source of livelihood to the fishing communities. On 14 October 1881 Eyemouth lost 129 of its men, almost the entire fishing fleet, in a terrific storm. They drowned in full sight of their watching families, smashed against the cliffs or on the shore. 'Eyemouth is a scene of unutterable woe,' lamented the Berwickshire News. 'The fleet is wrecked, and the flower of the fishermen have perished.' In the little town museum a tapestry woven by the townspeople in 1981, the centenary of the disaster, depicts these appalling events most movingly.

Around North Berwick the coast shifts from north to west and runs towards Edinburgh along the southern shore of the Firth of Forth. There are islands offshore, most of which can be visited by small boat when tide and weather are right. These are tiny 'worlds in the water'. By far the most dramatic is the Bass Rock, a craggy volcanic plug that rises like a massive round-topped pillar from the Forth's estuary a couple of miles off North Berwick. The Bass is as white as a wedding cake – not with

bird dung, as it first appears, but with birds themselves: 50,000 gannets, whose one and only east-coast stronghold this is. To stand in the heart of the squabbling, shrieking, flapping colony is an overwhelming experience. Further in along the estuary is the tiny causeway island of Cramond, where an 11th-century rival for the throne of Scotland was murdered by the king's brother. Opposite lies Inchcolm, an island pinched at the waist and rising to a knoll at each end, where splendid 12th-century monastic remains stand tall. The monastery was built by King Alexander I as a thanksgiving for deliverance from a storm in AD 1123, during which he had found himself stormbound on Inchcolm as the guest of the resident hermit.

Inland the Border market towns – Kelso, Melrose, Peebles, Jedburgh – are pleasant places, with an atmosphere of community and neighbourliness that many of their English counterparts have lost. They sit in the valleys of the rolling Southern Uplands, hills that

change character from the dark forests and pale grasses of Cheviot to broader, greener and more open vistas further north.

Ye maids o' high an' low degree
Frae Meggetdale tae Thornielee,
Kilt up your coats abune the knee
An' ower the hills tae Peebles.
As Beltane time comes roond each year
The exile, stirred by mem'ries dear,
Wad gie a wealth o' gowd an' gear
Tae spend a day in Peebles.

The Feast of Beltane, Mayday, has always provided Peebles folk with an excuse for a good rowdy festival. These days it takes place in June (to catch more tourists, naturally). Beltane Feast is a lively event, during which the Beltane Queen is crowned and the Beltane Cornet performs his ceremonial night-time jig in the High Street. There is a vigorous Riding of the Marches, too – a custom also observed at Lauder and several other Border towns – during which dozens of townsfolk of all ages turn out astride all kinds of horse-flesh, from hunters to hacks, and gallop in a thundering bunch around the borders of their lands.

Abbeys and castles dot this wide countryside, where for centuries the land-rich monasteries, beacons of learning and civilisation, were the only rivals to the authority and influence of the clan chiefs. A 50-mile (80-kilometre) walking trail, superbly beautiful, connects the four great ruined abbeys of Jedburgh (1138); Dryburgh (1150) in the Tweed Valley where the Lowlands' great novelist Sir Walter Scott lies in the north transept; Kelso (1128) with its graceful north transept; and Melrose (1136). As for the castles, they tend to be fortified houses rather than the conventional Norman-style stronghold. Thirteenth-century Neidpath on its crag above the River Tweed just outside Peebles is a good example, as is the slit-windowed 15th-century blockhouse of Barns Tower nearby. Along the Tweed Valley east of Peebles is the splendid conglomerate of Traquair House, a medieval tower house with bits and bobs added on through the centuries by the Maxwell Stuart owners to form a pleasing jumble of cellars, towers, arches, odd roof-lines, hidden rooms and passages. By contrast there is Abbotsford, the early-19th-century mock castle outside Melrose designed by Sir Walter Scott for himself, a fine romantic heap of turrets, battlements and frowning gable walls.

Further west along the Scottish Borders we come to the area around what was known as the Debatable Land, the land where no outside authority's writ ran and where might was right. Nithsdale, Annandale, Eskdale and Teviotdale are beautiful river valleys spreading like fingers north of the Solway Firth. On the high moors, upland lake valleys and wide hills between the rivers you can walk all day – all week, for that matter – and meet no one. Winters are wild here, summers wet, springs and autumns the seasons for big cloud-streaked skies and glowing colours of grass, moss and heather.

Into the valley of Moffat Water, east of Annandale, tumbles the Grey Mare's Tail, a 200-foot (61-metre) fall of water down a shiny black chute of rock. Not far away, a tremendous enclosed valley drops precipitously from the roadside – the Devil's Beef Tub, also known as the Marquis of Annandale's Beefstand from its former use as a hidey-hole for stolen cattle. 'It looks,' wrote Sir Walter Scott in *Redgauntlet*, 'as if four hills were laying their heads together, to shut out daylight from the dark hollow space between them. A d–d deep, black, black-guard-looking abyss of a hole it is, and goes straight down from the road-side, as perpendicular as it can do, to be a heathery brae. At the bottom, there is a small

ABOVE: Traquair House, riddled with secret rooms and crooked passageways, is the oldest continuously inhabited house in Scotland.

TOP: Gannets crowd the ledges of the Bass Rock, downriver from Edinburgh in the Firth of Forth. This 350-ft (107-m) volcanic plug looks as white as a wedding cake – not with guano, as one might think, but with the white bodies of the birds themselves, more than 50,000 of them. The Bass is the greatest stronghold of the gannet on the east coast of Britain.

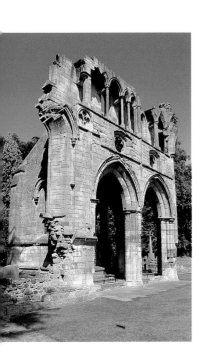

bit of a brook, that you would think could hardly find its way out from the hills that are so closely jammed round it.' That description still holds perfectly today.

South lies the wide Solway Firth and its apron of merses or salt marshes, where 20,000 barnacle geese arrive each autumn after a southward journey of 1,800 miles (3,000 kilometres) from Spitzbergen in the Arctic Circle. Watching them from one of the bird hides at Caerlaverock, especially at evening when they fly in gabbling packs of several thousand out to their night roosts on the Solway, is a literally breath-taking delight. West of Caerlaverock the coast runs in an endless succession of bays and mud flats, past the dusky sandstone town of Dumfries and the pretty inlet villages of Kirkcudbright (a kind of St Ives-on-Solway, much favoured by artists) and Gatehouse of Fleet, on

west towards Luce Bay and the hammerhead peninsula called the Rhinns of Galloway that forms the south-west tip of Scotland.

Galloway can lay claim to being the least-known corner of Scotland, a lonely circle of high moors, vast blankets of coniferous forest, sodden peat bogs and open-sided roads ribboning under immense skies. In Galloway Forest Park you can stand by Bruce's Stone, picturing the fugitive Robert Bruce in 1307 as he looked down on the braes around Loch Trool and watched his English enemies die under the boulders rolled down on them by his followers. It was a turning point in the Scots king's fortunes: from then on he would experience only success, crowned by the epic victory over Edward II, King of England, at Bannockburn in 1314. From Bruce's Stone a whole skein of walking trails penetrates the forest; some of the best and loneliest lead to remote hill ranges with tremendous names – the Awful Hand, the Dungeon – and up the nape of the highest peak around, the 2,766-foot (843-metre) Merrick.

From the Rhinns of Galloway the coast trends north, a great concave bow that curves for 80 miles (130 kilometres) around the Firth of Clyde before turning eastward down the Clyde to Glasgow. Tucked into the innermost hollow of this sandstone coast is Burns Country, the rural backwater around Ayr where Scotland's jealously adored national poet was born and

deep-fried Mars Bar. This cholesterol-rich delicacy, a chocolate-coated toffee bar dipped in batter and then fried in oil alongside more conventional pieces of fish, has given dozens of Glaswegians a premature taste of Heaven. There are some world-class galleries and museums in Glasgow, but it is rival Edinburgh that holds all the best scenic cards with its castle perched nobly on a crag, the basalt cliffs of Arthur's Seat, the great royal palace of Holyrood, and the handsome, wide streets and squares of the Georgian new town built below the Royal Mile and the medieval town.

spent most of his life. Relics and memorials of Robert Burns (1759–1796) are widespread: the cottage in Alloway where he was born on 25 January, pubs where he drank, such as Poosie Nansie's Tavern at Mauchline and the Tam O'Shanter in Ayr, and places featured in his poems: the Auld Brig of Ayr, Alloway Old Kirk where the tipsy hero of *Tam O'Shanter* blundered in on the witches' ball, and the Brig O'Doon where Tam's mare Maggie had her tail snatched off by a witch.

Along the tightly squeezed waist of Scotland lie her two chief cities, Glasgow and Edinburgh. Glasgow has grit and energy: a great shipbuilding and engineering city whose heavy industries are all but gone, looking at the future with confidence and characteristic humour. No one should pass through Glasgow without sampling the city's most famous culinary speciality – the

North of the Clyde and the Firth of Forth the feel of the country changes. Though this belt of Scotland is not really part of the Highlands, it is definitely nothing to do with the Borders. As for Lowlands – the hummocky Campsie Fells and the great wall of the Ochils at the gateway to Fife are scarcely low country. By far the best-known piece of country north of the two great cities is Loch Lomond, famous through the song about the 'bonnie, bonnie banks o' Loch Lomond'. The long, narrow lake under its guardian mountain of Ben Lomond is shaped like an elephant's head with a long trunk pointing north up Glen Falloch. Spattered with islets, lying under thickly wooded banks with the western flank of the Trossach hills beyond, it is a magnet for car-borne visitors from the city on summer weekends, but most truly lovely and free of crowds on a wintry weekday under clear skies. The

ABOVE: Snug little Kirkcudbright, haunt of artists and writers on the Solway Firth.

ABOVE: In this richly carved, bulging old Edinburgh house lived John Knox, 16th-century catalyst of the Scottish Reformation.

TOP: Robert Burns, the 'heaventaught ploughman' who became Scotland's national poet, was born in this humble cottage at Alloway, Ayrshire.

West Highland Way skirts its quieter eastern shore, to continue up Glen Falloch past the crash and roar of the Falls of Falloch. Dorothy Wordsworth came walking here with her brother William in the summer of 1802, and wrote up her impressions in her *Journal*:

We sate down, and heard, as if from the heart of the earth, the sound of torrents ascending out of the long glen ... it was everywhere, almost, one might say, as if "exhaled" through the whole surface of the green earth. Glenfalloch, Coleridge has since told me, signifies the Hidden Vale; but William says, if we were to name it from our recollections of that time, we should call it the Vale of Awful Sound.

East rise the Trossachs, mini-mountains where 19th-century citizens of Glasgow and Edinburgh flocked by railway and road to scramble up the peaks, go boating or cruising by steamer on Loch Katrine, and seek out Rob Roy's grave at Balquhidder. It was all thanks to Sir Walter Scott and his powerful gift for turning myth into historical fact. Not that there is any doubting the beauty and romance of such Trossach favourites as Ellen's Isle on Loch Katrine, or Inchmahome Island on the Lake of Menteith with the romantic ruins of a priory where Mary, Queen of Scots was hidden as a child in 1547 before being smuggled safely over the water to

France. Nor can the swashbuckling hero of Scott's *Rob Roy* easily be uncoupled from his real-life model, Red Robert MacGregor, a dashing cattle-thief and outlaw who throve in these parts around the turn of the 18th century. Rob Roy's graveslab in Balquidder churchyard is incised with a kilted man, a sword and a cross.

East again to Stirling, where one of the most striking castles in Scotland rises with unbeatable drama on the very summit of a 250-foot (75-metre) volcanic crag. Stirling Castle was the Royal Court of the Stuart monarchy for the last century-and-a-half of their rule in Scotland, and it stands guard over a charming small

town of cobbled streets and ancient tall houses. From the castle walls you look east to the abruptly rising rampart of the Ochil Hills, a wonderfully bare and impressive range that climbs in a green and brown wall from the valley of the River Devon. Halfway along, the flank of the range is pierced by the narrow Dollar Glen, up which you can climb on foot by way of the Burn of Care and the Burn of Sorrow to the dark ruin of Castle Gloom – names that truly give the atmosphere of this lonely spot.

Oh! Castell Gloom! thy strength is gane,
The green grass o'er thee growin',
On hill of Care thou art alane,

ABOVE: In winter the environs of Loch Lomond take on a harsh, steely quality. This is the season when Glaswegian walkers come out from the city to hike the hills around Loch Lomond, looking down over still, grey waters and frosty slopes.

LEFT: The 'bonnie, bonnie banks o' Loch Lomond'.

ABOVE: The Falls of Falloch tumble noisily through Glenfalloch north of Loch Lomond; William Wordsworth styled the glen 'the Vale of Awful Sound'.

The Sorrow round thee flowin'!
Oh! Castell Gloom! on thy fair wa's
Nae banners now are streamin';
The howlit flits amang the ha's,
And wild birds there are screamin'.

The castle was a Campbell stronghold, built in the 1490s. A Douglas who owned it was stabbed by no less an assailant than King James II of Scotland – quite an honour. It was burned by the flame-tipped arrows of a Maclean raiding party in 1654. A grim old tower, redolent with moody atmosphere: relic and symbol of so much bloody Lowland history. Out beyond the Ochils lies the Kingdom of Fife, not an autonomous realm but still a place pretty much apart. There are no dramas of landscape here; Fife is green and well-wooded farming country, with a southern coastline dotted with fishing villages. Like everywhere else around the shores of Britain, the fishing ports of Scotland have suffered economic decline as fish stocks dwindle and ever more stringent conservation measures are put in place. But in the East Neuk (eastern corner) of Fife the tradition is still extremely strong in harbour villages such as Pittenweem with its bustling early-morning fish market, and Anstruther whose excellent Scottish Fisheries Museum tells the story of this tough and demanding way of life.

ABOVE: Trying for a Trossach trout: the Lake of Menteith in early autumn.

RIGHT: Under the walls of the ancient castle of Stirling – a foundation at least 1,000 years old, perhaps twice that age – swordsmen try out their jousting skills during the annual Stirling Festival.

OPPOSITE: Stirling Castle, magnificently sited at the crest of a 250-ft (75-m) crag.

# 9

# THE HIGHLANDS AND THE ISLANDS

## WILD MOUNTAINS, GLENS AND SEA COASTS

ABOVE: The most photogenic castle in Scotland: the romantic island stronghold of Eilean Donan in the western Highlands.

OPPOSITE: Winter in the ill-famed Pass of Glencoe.

OVERLEAF: A picturebook Highland scene on Loch Leven.

THE CHALLENGE IS TO EXPLAIN exactly where the Highlands are. 'They are not the Lowlands' is the best one can say: a statement banal enough, but with a meaning quite obvious to anyone who knows Scotland. The Highlands and islands occupy the northernmost fifth of Britain. They contain only a tiny proportion of its population, and possess by far its most dramatic, lofty and wild landscape. For 300 years their people have been draining away to find a means of livelihood elsewhere. Now there is a trickle going the other way, deeper into the hills in search of peace, beauty, fresh air, unpolluted land and sea, solitude, a sense of stillness – all that the Highlands signify, in fact.

Along with the Lowlands and the Highlands, there ought to be a third title – the Westlands, maybe – for the wide-flung sprawl of sea-cut peninsulas that straggle south and west from the nape of Scotland's neck like the tattered mane of a horse. The southernmost of all, Kintyre, hangs south for 100 miles (161 kilometres), from where Inveraray Castle admires its own reflection in Loch Fyne. At the Mull of Kintyre, the southern tip of the Kintyre Peninsula, the splendid basalt cliffs of Northern Ireland's Antrim coast rise less than 15 miles (24 kilometres) off – twice as close, in fact, as the nearest point of mainland Scotland.

The ragged coast runs north by way of the Crinan Canal and the little ferry port of Oban (gateway to the islands of the Inner Hebrides), to penetrate Loch Linnhe towards Fort William. Just below the town rises the highest peak in Britain, the 4,406-foot (1,343-metre) Ben Nevis, an ill-shaped but impressive bulk dominating the north side of beautiful Glen Nevis.

Ten miles (16 kilometres) south of Fort William, the sea inlet of Loch Leven burrows east from Loch Linnhe. From the south shore of Loch Leven branches off the dark valley of Glencoe. Dark from the breaking wave of mountains that overhangs it, black and menacing in winter light or rainstorms; dark from its history, too. It was while staying as guests (albeit forcible ones) in the houses of the Macdonald clan that, at four in the morning of a bitter 13 February, 1692, Campbell of Glenlyon and his soldiers turned on their hosts and killed 38 of them – men, women and children. The Macdonalds fled into the snowbound hills, where several more died of wounds and exposure. The cause of the massacre was, ostensibly, the passing of a deadline for the clan chief, Macdonald of Glencoe, to swear allegiance to King William III. 'They must all be slaughtered,' were Campbell's orders. 'Put all to the sword under 70 ... see that the old fox and his cubs do on no account escape your hands.'

The treachery and savagery of the attack have ensured its enshrinement, not only in Scots nationalist hearts but in the general consciousness of the British. Glencoe is still a

name of ill-omen, its gloomy atmosphere reinforced by the brooding darkness of the glen. Rannoch Moor, a wide tract of weather-bitten heather moorland to the east of Glencoe, also partakes of this sombre character. Robert Louis Stevenson (1850–1894) used it to good effect as the setting for a manhunt adventure in his breathless novel *Kidnapped* (1886). The hero, David Balfour, has to crawl to safety across 'that country lying as waste as the sea; only the moor-fowl and the peewees crying upon it, and far over to the east, a herd of deer, moving like dots. Much of it was red with heather; much of the rest broken up with bogs and hags and peaty pools, some had been burned black in a heath fire; and in another place there was quite a forest of dead firs, standing like skeletons. A wearier-looking desert man never saw ...'

East again the ground steepens into fine mountains around Pitlochry and the upper reaches of the River

Tay. Here lies the snug small town of Aberfeldy, focus for tourists who climb to the beautiful waterfalls by which the Moness Burn descends to the Tay. Robert Burns came to view the falls in 1787, imported some imaginary 'birks' or birch trees through the power of poetic licence, and produced a verse description of the scene that still holds good:

The braes ascend like lofty wa's,
The foaming stream deep-roaring fa's,
O'erhung wi' fragrant spreading shaws,
The Birks o' Aberfeldy ...
The hoary cliffs are crowned wi' flowers
While o'er the linn the burnie pours,
And rising weet wi' misty showers,
The Birks o' Aberfeldy.

From Pitlochry the steep pass of Killiecrankie runs north-west past the splendid 13th-century Blair Castle, bristling with turrets and ranked windows, home of the Duke of Atholl who still maintains a private army and a personal piper. It was the Duke's ownership of the banks of the Bruar Water, a couple of miles upstream of Blair Castle, that prompted poet Burns to produce 'The Humble Petition of Bruar Water to the Noble Duke of Atholl' during his tour through this region. Burns regretted the absence of tree cover along the Bruar Water, a lack to which he tactfully drew the landowner's attention.

Here, foaming down the shelvy rocks,
In twisting strength I rin;
There, high my boiling torrent smokes,
Wild-roaring o'er a linn:
Enjoying large each spring and well
As Nature gave them me,
I am, although I say't mysel,
Worth gaun a mile to see.

Would then my noble master please
To grant my highest wishes,
He'd shade my banks wi' tow'rin trees,
And bonie spreading bushes.
Delighted doubly then, my Lord,
You'll wander on my banks,
And listen monie a grateful bird
Return you tuneful thanks.

The Bruar Water, like every other burn and river hereabouts, springs in the high massif of the Cairngorm Mountains, Scotland's winter playground, a harsh granite ring of peaks that rise at their highest to over 4,000 feet (1,219 metres). Conditions up here can literally be arctic; winds and blizzards can turn ferocious. Lives are lost each year as under-experienced or ill-equipped walkers, skiers and climbers make fatal misjudgements. The Cairngorms are not to be fooled with. But they offer wonderfully exciting scenery and every kind of outdoor challenge within a small compass. Ptarmigan, golden eagle, red deer, wild cat and winter-white mountain hare live their stealthy lives up here. Walkers can venture into the high massif in guided parties from outdoor centres such as Glenmore Forest Park near Aviemore, the unpicturesque but functional capital of the Cairngorms. Or they can go in small independent parties if they have enough experience. Either way, the walking is memorably exhilarating.

Out of the heart of the Cairngorms flows the River Dee, descending to carve out a most beautiful valley as it runs east to the sea at Aberdeen. This is Royal Deeside, country beloved of the Royal Family since Queen Victoria and Prince Albert bought the Balmoral

RIGHT: Herds of wild red deer roam the slopes and glens of the Highlands and islands.

LEFT: Mountain hares are a rare sight, but a memorable one – especially in winter, if one is lucky enough to spot one sprinting in its snowy white winter coat across a dark scree or rocky slope.

BELOW: A flock of ptarmigan in their white winter plumage.

ABOVE: Busbies, sporrans and bagpipes: Scottish soldiers make formal battle music.

BELOW: Queen Victoria and her consort Prince Albert bought the Balmoral estate in 1852; most of present-day Balmoral Castle was built to Albert's designs.

estate on the banks of the Dee in 1852. Balmoral Castle, country home of the monarch while in Scotland, is only one of the royalty-related attractions along the Dee Valley. Among these are Braemar, where the Royal Family attends the orgy of caber-tossing, wrestling in kilts and hammer-throwing at the annual Highland Games; also Ballater with its restored station often used by royalty in the past, and modest (though sizeable) Crathie Church, where kings and queens have worshipped and continue to do so. Even without the royal connection, though, Deeside would be magnetically attractive to visitors with its trees, water and shapely flanking hills.

Of a different character is the River Spey, a sparkling salmon river that widens as it winds north from Cairngorm towards the sea. The Spey is bright, lively, fast-flowing and full of colour, like the famous tune 'The Spey In Spate', which was composed in its honour and is so descriptive of its hurry and noise when in spring flood. Near Boat of Garten, ospreys nest and rear their young in early summer on a jealously guarded nature reserve. Below here the Spey passes a whole string of small distilleries – Glenlivet, Glenfiddich, Macallan, Knockando, Tamdhu and others – whose private burns, tributaries of the Spey, flow through peat to produce a flavour and quality of water that is ideal for the production of single malt whiskies. Salmon fishermen stand in their waders waist-deep in the Spey, intent on landing one of the river's famed 60-pounders (27 kilograms), elegantly casting their flies with a pinpoint accuracy that looks easy until you try it. Down at Speymouth the river rushes loudly between shingle banks past the old and evocatively named net-fishing community of Tugnet, before mingling its oxygen-crammed fresh water with the cold salt of Moray Firth. A freshly caught wild salmon is a rare table treat; and there are plenty more delicacies harvested from the great outdoors to be enjoyed in this part of Scotland. Game is the name up here – venison, grouse, pheasant, sea trout – as well as scallops and seafood gathered by inshore boats.

Like a deep wound carved with a straight-bladed knife, the Great Glen cuts the Highlands of Scotland neatly in two. A geological fault, it forms an undeviating, 70-mile (113-kilometre) channel running southwest from Inverness on the Moray Firth to Fort William on Loch Linnhe. Most famous of its features is the long, narrow basin of Loch Ness, in whose peat-darkened waters the rumours of 1,500 years have located a water monster. Could it be some pre-Ice Age colony of creatures, trapped here for ever more? Or is the whole thing a load of over-hyped twaddle? A

1930s snapshot 'by a passing motorist' shows what could be a blurred head and neck emerging from the water. A few years ago there were photos in the papers, purportedly taken in Loch Ness by underwater camera, of the large rhombus-shaped fin of some submarine beast. Sir Peter Scott, the eminent naturalist, was reported to have named the creature *nessiteras rhombopteryx*. Very authentic-sounding – until someone pointed out that this was an anagram of 'monster hoax by Sir Peter S' ...

North and west of the Great Glen is the heart of the Highlands, the wild, mountainous land stripped so brutally of its inhabitants during the Highland Clearances of the 18th and 19th centuries, when landlords replaced their tenants – and a whole Gaelic culture and way of life – with more profitable sheep.

There is tremendous grandeur and natural beauty about these vast, empty tracts of mountain, glen and sea coast; also a pervasive melancholy that anyone with a feeling for Scottish history must sense.

Down in the south-west of the region is a cluster of very sparsely populated Atlantic peninsulas. Morvern faces the Isle of Mull. Ardgour and Sunart lead to craggy Ardnamurchan, Moidart and Morar. Out around remote Knoydart the coastal communities are more easily reached by boat than by road. North again is Kyle of Lochalsh; from here the spectacular line of the Dingwall and Skye Railway runs north-east up Glen Carron in wonderful mountain scenery towards Inverness.

This region is Wester Ross, thinly populated, deeply cut with rugged sea lochs, visited with wild weather in winter, mild enough in summer to allow subtropical

ABOVE: The whitewashed croft house is still a common sight throughout the Highlands. Along with the house goes a few acres of land, good or bad according to the district: enough to provide a living for a family in simpler times, but generally producing only a small part of a crofter's income these days.

gardens to flourish at Inverewe. North again is
Sutherland, lumped with back-of-the-ranges mountains
and a savage coast that turns abruptly east around the
aptly named Cape Wrath. From here the British mainland's northernmost outpost narrows slowly as one
enters Caithness, a region whose soft heart, composed
of a giant blanket bog, lies enclosed in a hard shell of
old red sandstone cliffs. The area around the great bog,
known as the Flow Country, has been threatened for
decades by commercial forestry and peat-cutting. Only
recently has this dour region been recognised as a
unique community of plant and animal life. Ninety-
eight percent of the bog is water. Only the uppermost
couple of inches is firm ground, and even that quakes
and squelches like a jellified sponge as you walk
across it. The million-acre (404,000-hectare) blanket
of sphagnum moss and other bog-forming plants
sustains a wonderfully varied community of inhabitants: water beetles, dragonflies, frogs, wild cat, deer,
otter, black-throated divers, greenshank and golden

plover; lousewort, sundew, dozens of lichen species,
mosses, fragrant bog myrtle. A magical, rich-smelling,
enchanting place.

Beyond runs the northernmost coast. Duncansby
Head is the place to stand, out beyond famed John
O'Groats at the very tip of mainland Britain, where
dark cliffs plunge away into a whirl of rocks and
water. From here you can gaze across the wind-
whipped waters of the Pentland Firth. If you are
lucky, the sea spray and low cloud will be thin enough
to give you a glimpse of low-lying islands out there:
Stroma and South Ronaldsay, the southern edge of
the Orkney archipelago.

Scotland's great 500-mile (800-kilometre) chain of
offshore islands is divided into three distinct sections.
The Inner Hebrides curl close in around the mainland's west coast. Thirty miles (50 kilometres) further
out into the Atlantic lie the Outer Hebrides or Western
Isles, a scimitar-shaped chain 130 miles (200 kilometres) long which shadows the north-easterly curve of

the mainland. The two neighbouring archipelagos of Orkney and Shetland, collectively known as the Northern Isles, chase each other north from the north-eastern tip of mainland Scotland.

Of the Inner Hebrides, Islay and Jura represent the southernmost full stop. Lying west of the Kintyre Peninsula, they are roughly on a level with Glasgow. On a level ... but in a different world. Thinly populated, with their west coasts deeply sea-bitten, covered in hilly peat bog, they are a pair of beautiful wild twins. Their whisky is strong, deep golden and flavoured tarrily with peat smoke. Greenland white-fronted geese vie with the distillery furnaces for possession of the peat mosses of Islay: for the geese, the attraction lies in the nutritious roots of bog cotton and white beak-sedge. The jury is still out on this confrontation between the forces of commercialism and conservation. On neighbouring Jura (where George Orwell wrote 1984, relishing the island peace), red deer outnumber humans by twenty to one.

North lies the big island of Mull, a layered dome of basalt. Red deer are rampant here, too, unculled residents of shooting estates too expensive to maintain these days. Three ragged peninsulas grope westward, like the tentacles of some sea creature. Ardmeanach, the middle one, is the wildest, with a rough and thrilling track to follow round its cliffs. South sprawls the Ross of Mull peninsula, ending at Fionnphort, where a little ferry buzzes you across in five minutes to the holy island of Iona. Here you find a beautifully restored Abbey, headquarters and spiritual home of the world-wide interdenominational Iona Community. St Columba is their inspiration: a 6th-century Irish monk on the run, who landed on Iona in AD 563 and lit a torch of faith that blazed from this tiny island for 1000 years. Nearly 50 Scottish kings lie buried here, and uncounted holy men and women. Iona is beautiful, rugged and green, its western beaches spattered with sea-green marble and pink granite.

From Iona boats go out to Staffa, volcanic rock's architectural masterpiece with its tall, black hexagonal

ABOVE: Highland cattle browse contentedly on seaweed near Duart Castle in the Isle of Mull.

RIGHT: Iona Abbey: St Columba founded a Celtic Christian culture here that spread and flourished for 1000 years.

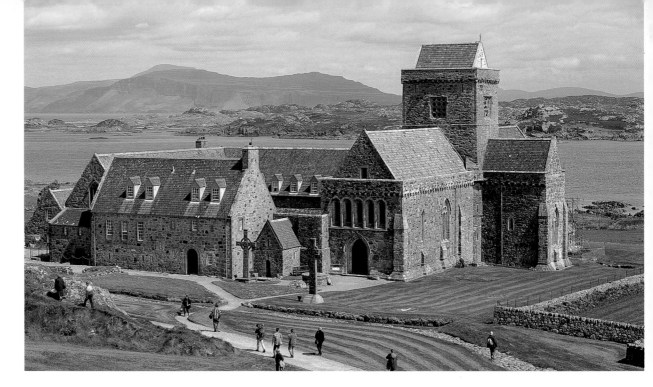

BELOW: The hills of Skye, most romantic of Scottish islands.

columns and bulging, brain-like basalt topping. You can nose into the vaulted, cathedral-like cavern of Fingal's Cave where Felix Mendelssohn came in 1829, conquering a bout of swell-induced seasickness to grasp inspiration for his *Hebridean Overture*. Up on the summit of Staffa grow outsize orchids, vetches and ragged robin, all thriving in deep, grassy sward enriched by wind-deposited shell sand.

From Staffa you look out west beyond the surfacing submarine shapes of the Treshnish Islands (more basaltic extravaganzas) to see the twin islands of Coll and Tiree lying low on the horizon. On craggy Coll, rare corncrakes breed in late-cut grasslands; on sister Tiree the grass is short and wind-bitten, superb grazing for cattle who munch a floral salad as the eternal sea wind rakes their fields.

North again to visit Rhum, Muck and Eigg, the euphonically styled Cocktail Isles. It would be hard to find three more notably contrasted islands. Rhum is diamond-shaped and mountainous, a 26,000-acre (10,522-hectare) nature reserve where golden eagles, white-tailed sea eagles, merlin, red-throated divers and dozens of other bird species thrive, along with a large herd of red deer and communities of alpine plants that have been here for 10,000 years. There is an eccentric castle, too, built for the rich Bullough family from Lancashire to live in as they pursued a lairdly rôle on Rhum around the turn of the 20th century. Now the Bulloughs lie in a Greek temple of a mausoleum on a remote shore under the mountain peaks, stately in death.

Muck, to the south, is a tiny, roundish button of an island, whose population of 30 work hard and successfully to farm, fish and maintain their precious community spirit. Eigg, on the other hand, became the run-down plaything of one rich eccentric after

ABOVE: Looking from Ardtoe's white sands on the coast of Moidart towards the basalt cliffs of the Isle of Eigg and the mountains of Rhum beyond.

another, until in 1998 the islanders bought their island for themselves and set about putting its deteriorated economy and social life on a sounder footing. Eigg is a strangely shaped place. A giant curtain of basalt crags curves well over 1,000 feet (305 metres) high at its northern end, and a great volcanic whalehead looms to 1,300 feet (396 metres) down at the other end. In the cliffs below, a tiny hole and a crouching passage lead to a cave. Here the entire Macdonald population of Eigg crawled into hiding in 1577 when a party of Macleods from Harris mounted a raid on the island. Every man, woman and child was smothered to death when the Macleods lit a smoky fire at the entrance. Three hundred and ninety-five people died. Grim doings, the very stuff of island history.

Skye, of course, is the queen of all the Inner Hebrides: the biggest, the grandest and by far the best known – mostly thanks to the romantic tale of Bonnie Prince Charlie and Flora Macdonald. The young woman from the island of South Uist acted as guide and companion to the ill-fated Charles Stewart, defeated Pretender to the throne, as he was rowed 'over the sea to Skye' in June 1746 during his escape to France after the disastrous rebellion he had fronted the year before.

Skye is connected to the mainland at Kyle of Lochalsh by a bridge these days: a modern facility sadly injurious to romance, but a good practical way of getting visitors and locals on and off the island. The five great peninsulas of Skye – Trotternish, Vaternish, Duirinish, Minginish and Sleat – stretch out west like the fingers of a misshapen hand. From the palm of the hand rise the splendid, harsh shapes of the Cuillin Hills. An immense basalt cliff forms the spine of Trotternish in the north; Dunvegan Castle of the Macleods out west, and Armadale of the Macdonalds in the south, are impressive old strongholds; there are glorious views in every corner of Skye. But it is the Cuillins that form the heart of the place, 3,000 feet

ABOVE: Pristine beach on the west coast of Lewis in the Outer Hebrides.

OPPOSITE: Mighty basalt crags at The Quiraing on the Trotternish Peninsula, Isle of Skye.

(914 metres) in the air, their hard outlines stamped against an ice-blue sky, smoking with dark cloud or softly lit through a wavering curtain of rain.

A journey through the Western Isles will take you through scenes of stunning beauty, most of a bleak and weatherbeaten nature. A scatter of tiny islands – among them Mingulay, famous through the 'Mingulay Boat Song' – leads north to Barra, the chief island in the southern quarter of the chain. The population is mostly Roman Catholic; almost all speak Gaelic, many as their first language, in this outpost archipelago where the ancient language has been kept alive against all the odds. South and North Uist lead north, islands fragmented by countless lochs and inlets, with mountainous east coasts and western shores flattening into the lush, flowery sward called *machair*, built up on lime-rich shell sand. Between the two Uists lies square little Benbecula, an island more liquid than solid, as flat as a pancake except for the 400-foot (122-metre) pimple of Rueval. From North Uist a ferry ride brings you to Harris, where the mountains suddenly rise in earnest. Harris is famous above all for homespun tweed – an increasingly rare and highly priced commodity these days, but there are still a few producers of the genuine article on the island. Most prized of all is tweed dyed with colours prepared from Harris's native plants; you can expect to pay

a small fortune for this. Harris shades strangely into Lewis with no sea barrier. Lewis, the northernmost of the Western Isles, is also the biggest, a 40-mile (64-kilometre) blunt spearhead of bog and loch, hill and peat hag, where ancient stones stand in circles and lonely roads run for miles to disused fishing quays. Up at the northernmost tip of the island you can climb to the top of the lighthouse at the Butt of Lewis. From the viewing platform, 200 feet (61 metres )in the air, you will get a memorable view over land and sea. You can't buy a drink on Sunday in Lewis, a stronghold of the ultra-conservative Free Presbyterian Church, but you can spit a long way before hitting a teetotaller. It takes time and a good eye to appreciate this storm-battered, windy, rainswept island, and the warm hearts and indomitable community spirit that sustain it. Forty miles (64 kilometres) further into the Atlantic rises tiny St Kilda, depopulated in the 1930s and now an army radar tracking station – as wild, lonely and stormy an island as one could imagine.

Out across the Pentland Firth from Duncansby Head, the Orkney archipelago is founded on warm red sandstone. It keeps the fields green and lush, though not many trees can stand against the salt wind up here. The Norse influence is strong – in the architecture of the big chambered tombs, the look of the carved faces on the stones of St Magnus's Cathedral in Kirkwall, the fair colour of cheeks and hair that you see all round you. Mainland is the chief island, with red sandstone Kirkwall its capital. Star archaeological attractions of Mainland include the four Stones of Stenness, erected some 5,000 years ago, and the nearby Ring of Brodgar, 1,000 years younger, its 30 stones thin and straight-sided, some sharply cut on an angle at the top, many of them double human height. As for prehistoric tombs, the star is Maes Howe, a green hillock in a field that conceals an astonishing chamber built of fitted stones around 3,000 BC. Some of the great stones are scored with spidery runes, graffiti left by Vikings who plundered Maes Howe of whatever treasures had been buried there over the millennia. Out on the western shore of Mainland lies Skara Brae, a complete Neolithic village

excavated from a sand dune – stone tables, beds, benches and shelves perfectly preserved within the tiny houses.

Exploring the archipelago, you come across many other archaeological treasures. In South Ronaldsay's Tomb of the Eagles, human remains were found mixed mysteriously with the feathers of sea eagles. A mighty 24-seater chambered tomb on Rousay, known as the 'Ship of Death', stands on the shore next to the stump of a sturdy Iron Age broch, or defensive tower. At the Knap of Howar on tiny Papa Westray, a pair of 5,500-year-old semi-detached houses stand on a remote and beautiful shore.

Orkney is not all archaeology, of course. The sea has carved some tremendous sculptures in the islands' sandstone, champion of all being the giant sea stack

BELOW: Stone Age houses, perfectly preserved in sand drifts at Skara Brae on Orkney Mainland.

low-lying and windswept. As in Orkney, the chief island is known as Mainland. Two more sizeable islands, Yell and Unst, lie in line to the north, with smaller off-islands scattered in the sea around.

There are few rich dairying farms here. The land is too harsh, too beaten about by the North Sea weather. The Shetland archipelago, 70 miles (113 kilometres) from toe to tip, looks blown into rags when seen on the map. The sea has bitten its flanks so deeply that nowhere in Shetland is more than 3 miles (5 kilometres) from the sea. At certain points, for example at Mavis Grind – a narrow neck of land halfway up the Mainland island – the saying is that you can throw a pebble from the North Sea to the Atlantic. These are sea-worn and sea-dominated islands.

There are fine archaeological remains in Shetland. The most notable is the excavated settlement of Jarlshof, near Sumburgh airport at the southern tip of Mainland, where Bronze Age dwellings, Iron Age wheelhouses, Norse longhouses, medieval farms and nobles' mansions lie squashed into a layer-cake of history. Another five-star site is the really superb Pictish broch, or stone tower, on the island of Mousa, 45 feet (14 metres) high and unquestionably the best-preserved broch in Britain.

Marine wildlife is abundant here – seals, whales, dolphins, seabirds in their millions. World-famous bird reserves include Hermaness on the northernmost headland of Unst, the very forehead of Britain, and tiny Fair Isle halfway between Orkney and Shetland. Then there is the spectacular coastline, carved by the savage power of the sea. Also, of course, the legendary hospitality of the Shetlanders, and the fiery delights of their fiddle music and island dances. A constant element in the landscape is peat-reek, the sweet smell of peat harvested from the bog in the traditional way with a narrow-bladed spade known in Shetland as a 'tushkar'. You'll see the low ramparts of the islanders' peat banks everywhere you go. Peat, once properly dried, burns slow and hot, and makes the ideal fire to sit beside with a glass of malt whisky while someone plays a Shetland reel on the fiddle.

The time at which all these elements best come together is on the last Tuesday every January, in the depths of a wild North Sea winter, when Shetland holds its great midwinter celebration of Up-Helly-Aa. As 800 flaring torches go streaming flame through the snowy streets of the archipelago's capital, Lerwick, and dozens of ferociously yelling, bush-bearded Norsemen set fire to a full-size longship and watch her blaze before embarking on a night's drinking and dancing, you see the spirit of these islands burning at its maddest and brightest.

ABOVE: A Viking longship erupts in flame, the culmination of Shetland's midwinter celebration of Up-Helly-Aa.

TOP: Three thousand years of human habitation are on display at the Jarlshof excavations in Shetland Mainland.

known as the Old Man of Hoy, which towers unsupported off the north-west coast of the island of Hoy to an incredible height of 450 feet (137 metres).

Orkney social life is legendary. Visitors to any island should be prepared to be included at the drop of a hat in whatever music, dancing and general hospitality may be going on. And that also applies, in spades, to Orkney's sister archipelago of Shetland, the most northerly islands in Britain.

Shetland's foundations are of more ancient rock than Orkney. These islands are peat-blanketed, treeless,

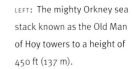
LEFT: The mighty Orkney sea stack known as the Old Man of Hoy towers to a height of 450 ft (137 m).

# A Selection of Walkways and Routes

One of the best ways to get to know rural Britain and its people is to go out and explore the countryside on foot. Britain boasts the densest network of public rights of way in the world, beautifully and accurately charted on the 1:50,000 Landranger and 1:25,000 Explorer and Outdoor Leisure maps of the Ordnance Survey (OS). All walkers are free to invent their own walking routes by using these footpaths; but for those who would like the planning work done for them, hundreds of excellent walks have already been established and waymarked, and are carefully maintained in good condition. The longer paths are especially rewarding to follow, as you can either walk a section and then loop back to your starting point on another nearby footpath, or you can complete several dozen miles over a few days.

Here is a selection of some of the most enjoyable of Britain's longer footpaths.

## Cleveland Way

This 110-mile (177-kilometre) path starts in the large, lively village of Helmsley in the North York Moors National Park, and makes a great clockwise loop around the perimeter of the North York Moors before turning south to run down the spectacular coastline of North Yorkshire as far as the headland of Filey Brigg. Sherpa Van (020 8569 4101) will carry your luggage between night stops; OS Landrangers 93, 94, 99, 100 and 101 are the maps you need.

## Ridgeway/Icknield Way/Peddar's Way

Three ancient trackways that form a continuous walk of around 250 miles (402 kilometres) across southern England and East Anglia. The Ridgeway (85 miles [137 kilometres]; OS Landrangers 165, 173, 174, 175), some 5,000 years old, runs along the chalk ridge from Overton Hill near the prehistoric stone monuments of Avebury in Wiltshire to Ivinghoe Beacon, Buckinghamshire, the highest point of the Chiltern Hills. From Ivinghoe Beacon it continues eastwards as the Icknield Way (105 miles [169 kilometres]; OS Landrangers 144, 154, 155, 165, 166), an equally ancient route which comes to Knettishall Heath on the Norfolk/Suffolk border near Thetford. Here it swings north-west along the historic Peddar's Way (50 miles [80 kilometres]; OS Landrangers 142, 132) to reach the Norfolk coast at Holme-next-the-Sea.

## North Downs Way/Pilgrim's Way

A path along the beautifully wooded ridge of the North Downs south of London, which runs for 140 miles (225 kilometres) from Farnham on the Surrey/ Hampshire border to Dover on the coast of Kent. It keeps close company within the Pilgrim's Way, an ancient route used by medieval pilgrims travelling from Winchester to St Thomas à Becket's tomb in Canterbury Cathedral. OS Landrangers 178, 179, 186, 187, 188, 189.

## South Downs Way

Superb 105-mile (169-kilometre) bridleway-cum-footpath along the rounded backs of the South Downs from Winchester to Eastbourne; probably the best bet for anyone inexperienced at long-distance walking. OS Landrangers 185, 197, 198, 199.

## Offa's Dyke

Wonderfully exhilarating rollercoaster of a walk, 180 miles (290 kilometres) along the rolling, castle-dotted country of the Welsh Borders, based on the route of an 8th-century earthwork. Landscape and history interwoven. OS Landrangers 116, 117, 126, 137, 148, 161, 162.

## West Highland Way

Some of Scotland's most striking scenery – mountains, glens, lochs and moors – unfolds on this 95-mile (153-kilometre) journey from Milngavie ('Mul-guy') on the northern outskirts of Glasgow to Fort William in the shadow of Ben Nevis. Highlights include Loch Lomond, the Falls of Falloch, wild Rannoch Moor and the Devil's Staircase, and memorable views of Glencoe. You'll need OS 1:25,000 Outdoor Leisure 38, 39; Sherpa Van (020 8569 4101) or Travel-Lite (0141 956 7890, spring and summer only) will transport your luggage between overnight stops.

## Pennine Way

The Daddy of them all – nearly 260 miles (420 kilometres) of wild, wet and windy, but magnificently bleak and beautiful Pennine country, on a path notorious for its peaty, muddy muckiness that storms up the spine of England in grand style from Edale in Derbyshire to Kirk Yetholm just across the Scottish Border. Completing the Pennine Way is a challenge for experienced hill-walkers, but you can devise endless circular walks based on this truly outstanding National Trail.

## Coast-to-Coast

An increasingly popular route, 190 miles (306 kilometres) long, that crosses the north of England from St Bees on the coast of western Cumbria to Robin Hood's Bay on the Yorkshire coast. It takes in some beautiful Lake District scenery, bleak Pennine landscape, the Yorkshire Dales and the dourly characterful North York Moors. Best maps are the OS's Outdoor Leisure strip maps 33, 34. Sherpa Van (020 8569 4101) or Coast to Coast Baggage Service (01642 489173) will carry your pack between overnight stops.

# ORGANISATIONS

BRITISH TOURIST AUTHORITY
Useful website that includes details of accommodation, events, places to visit, travel information, activities, attractions, and more.
ADDRESS Thames Tower, Black's Road, London W6 9EL
TEL NO. 020 8846 9000
WEBSITE www.visitbritain.com

BRITISH WATERWAYS
Operate the canals and inland waterways, and can advise on waterborne holidays, fishing and canal towpath walking.
ADDRESS Willow Grange, Church Road, Watford, Hertfordshire WD1 3QA
TEL NO. 01923 226422
WEBSITE HYPERLINK http://www.britishwaterways.co.uk www.britishwaterways.co.uk

CAMPING AND CARAVANNING CLUB
Explorers on a tight budget can expect high standards anywhere that displays this sign.
ADDRESS Greenfields House, Westwood Way, Coventry CV4 8JH
TEL NO. 01203 694995
WEBSITE HYPERLINK http://www.camping www.campingandcaravanningclub.co.uk

COUNCIL FOR THE PROTECTION OF RURAL ENGLAND (CPRE)
Watchdog group that keeps government and local authorities up to the mark, as its name implies.
ADDRESS Warwick House, 25 Buckingham Palace Road, London SW1W 0PP
TEL NO. 020 7976 6433
WEBSITE www.cpre.org.uk

COUNCIL FOR THE PROTECTION OF RURAL WALES (CPRW)
ADDRESS Ty Gwyn , 31 High Street, Welshpool, Powys SY21 7YD
TEL NO. 01938 552525
WEBSITE www.cprw.org.uk

COUNTRYSIDE AGENCY
Government agency charged with ensuring that various groups with an interest in the countryside – farmers, walkers, local inhabitants, rural businesses etc. – work together and not against one another.
ADDRESS John Dower House, Crescent Place, Cheltenham GL50 3RA
TEL NO. 01242 521381
WEBSITE www.countryside.gov.uk

COUNTRYSIDE COUNCIL FOR WALES
Does for Wales what the Countryside Agency does for England.
ADDRESS Plas Penrhos, Ffordd Penrhos, Bangor, Gwynedd LL57 2LQ
TEL NO. 01248 385500
WEBSITE www.ccw.gov.uk

ENGLISH HERITAGE
Cares for some of the finest historic buildings in England.
ADDRESS 23 Savile Row, London W1X 1AB
TEL NO. 020 7973 3434
WEBSITE www.english-heritage.org.uk

ENGLISH NATURE
Its former title of the Nature Conservancy Council describes its role; the organisation owns and runs many nature reserves around England.
ADDRESS Northminster House, Peterborough, Cambridgeshire PE1 1UA
TEL NO. 01733 455100
WEBSITE www.english-nature.org.uk

FORESTRY COMMISSION
This organisation has responsibility for the nationally owned forests of Britain; part of its duty is to exploit them commercially, but its other role is to promote leisure use of the forests through walking and cycling trails, information points, picnic areas, ranger-led expeditions, and so on.
ADDRESS 231 Corstophine Road, Edinburgh EH12 7AT
TEL NO. 0131 334 4473
WEBSITE www.forestry.gov.uk

LANDMARK TRUST

Owns some spectacularly strange follies, lighthouses, towers and even an island, which it hires out for holiday use.

ADDRESS Shottesbrooke, Maidenhead, Berkshire SL6 3SW

TEL NO. 01628 825920

WEBSITE www.landmarktrust.co.uk

NATIONAL TRUST

The organisation that cares for land and buildings of national interest and importance, either bought by the Trust or given to it by private owners.

ADDRESS 36 Queen Anne's Gate, London SW1H 9AS

TEL NO. 020 7222 9251

WEBSITE www.nationaltrust.org.uk

NATIONAL TRUST FOR SCOTLAND

ADDRESS 28 Charlotte Street, Edinburgh EH2 4ET

TEL NO. 0131 243 9300

WEBSITE www.nts.org.uk

ORDNANCE SURVEY

Recent private competition has made this once-complacent state mapping organisation look to its laurels. The 1:50,000 and 1:25,000 maps it produces are still the best in the world for walkers, cyclists and other countryside explorers.

ADDRESS Romsey Road, Maybush, Southampton SO16 4GU

TEL NO. 02380 792912

WEBSITE www.ordsvy.gov.uk

RAMBLERS' ASSOCIATION

A very powerful lobby and ginger group with 100,000 members, which campaigns vigorously on behalf of the walker.

ADDRESS 1–5 Wandsworth Road, London SW8 2XX

TEL NO. 020 7821 3046

WEBSITE www.ramblers.org.uk

ROYAL SOCIETY FOR THE PROTECTION OF BIRDS (RSPB)

A long-established pressure group, dedicated to the welfare of birds, which owns and runs some superb bird reserves.

ADDRESS The Lodge, Sandy, Bedfordshire SG19 2DL

TEL NO. 01767 680551

WEBSITE www.rspb.org.uk

SCOTTISH NATURAL HERITAGE

ADDRESS Battleby, Redgorton, Perth PH1 3EW

TEL NO. 01738 444177

WEBSITE www.snh.org.uk

SUSTRANS (SUSTAINABLE TRANSPORT)

Admirable organisation dedicated to creating and maintaining walking and cycling routes, many along disused railways.

ADDRESS 35 King Street, Bristol BS1 4DZ

TEL NO. 0117 927 7555

WEBSITE www.sustrans.org.uk

WILDFOWL AND WETLAND TRUST

Founded by famous naturalist and wildfowl painter Sir Peter Scott, the WWT runs several wetland reserves in the UK.

ADDRESS Slimbridge, Gloucestershire GL2 7BT

TEL NO. 01453 890333

WEBSITE www.wwt.org.uk

WILDLIFE TRUSTS

County-based organisations, supported (and often sustained) by dedicated volunteers, who run reserves, organise activities and promote sensitive understanding and enjoyment of wildlife.

ADDRESS The Kiln, Waterside, Mather Road, Newark, Nottinghamshire NG24 1WT

TEL NO. 01636 677711

WEBSITE www.wildlifetrusts.org.uk

YOUTH HOSTEL ASSOCIATION (YHA)

Long-standing self-help group that runs cheap but comfortable accommodation for walkers and other country-goers on a tight budget.

ADDRESS Trevelyan House, 8 St Stephens Hill, St Alban's, Hertfordshire AL1 2DY

TEL NO. 01727 855215

WEBSITE www.org.uk

# GLOSSARY

## PLACE-NAMES

SAXON/OLD ENGLISH

-burgh or -bury (Glastonbury)
= large farm or manor house

-ham (Parham) = flat pasture or meadow near a river

-wick (Randwick) = cattle or sheep farm

-ley (Warley) = a clearing or forest glade

-ing (Goring) = place of the followers
of the original settler

-ton (Middleton) = settlement on open ground
above a river

NORSE

-beck (Pinchbeck) = place by a stream

-by (Somerby) = farm

-thwaite (Langthwaite) = clearing or meadow

-garth (Aysgarth) = enclosed ground

-dale (Swaledale) = valley

-setter (Langsetter) = summer upland dwelling

## HISTORICAL PERIODS

**Stone Age**  $c.6000$ BC – $c.2000$ BC

**Bronze Age**  $c.2000$ BC – $c.600$ BC

**Iron Age**  $c.600$ BC – AD 43

**Roman Britain**  AD 43 – $c.$ AD 410

**Dark Ages/Anglo-Saxon**  $c.$ AD 450 – 1066

**Viking raiding and settling**  $c.800$ – $c.1100$

**Norman**  1066 – 1154

**Middle Ages/medieval England**  roughly 1066–1485,
the period between the Norman Conquest and the Tudors

**Wars of the Roses**  1455–1485 – civil war, between the
Houses of York and Lancaster, for the English throne

**Tudor**  1485–1603

**Reformation**  1533–1540, when King Henry VIII
founded the Church of England, abolished the British

monasteries and sold off their buildings, property
and land

**Elizabethan**  during the reign of Queen Elizabeth I,
1558–1603

**Jacobean**  during the reign of King James I, 1603–1625

**Queen Anne**  during the reign of Queen Anne,
1702–1714

**Georgian**  1714–1830, during the consecutive reigns
of King George I, II, III and IV

**Industrial Revolution**  mid-18th to mid-19th century,
when first water- and then steam-powered
manufacturing made Britain the 'Workshop of the World'

**Regency**  1811–1820, when George, Prince of Wales
ruled the country because his father, King George III,
was suffering periods of insanity

**Victorian**  during the reign of Queen Victoria,
1837–1901

**Edwardian**  during the reign of King Edward VII,
1901–1910

## ARCHITECTURAL TERMS

**barrow**  prehistoric burial mound

**boss**  decorative projection, usually where ribs
of vaulting meet

**box pews**  high-sided enclosed pews, typical
of pre-Victorian churches

**broch**  Iron Age cylindrical defensive stone tower, unique
to Scotland

**chambered tomb**  Stone Age tomb divided into
compartments

**chapter house**  meeting place for the canons
of a cathedral or members of a monastic order

**clerestory**  row of second-storey windows,
high in the walls of a church nave

**corbel stone**  projecting from a wall, often carved,
supporting roof, beam or another feature

**crypt**  space below the floor of a church, usually under
the east end

**dormer window** window standing out from a roof

**flushwork** decorative work with flint, juxtaposed with stonework

**Gothic** architecture typical of the period from *c*.1190 to Tudor times, using the pointed arch and varying from the comparative simplicity of Early English to the elaborations of the Decorative style

**half-timbered** timber-framed

**hammerbeam roof** a roof supported on hammerbeams, which are rows of horizontal timbers projecting towards each other from the top of opposite walls; they do not meet in the middle, but end in vertical timbers which rise to an arched beam that forms the apex of the roof

**Martello towers** thick-walled oval towers similar to brochs (see above); a chain of these was built up the eastern coast of Britain from 1803, to guard against invasion by the troops of Napoleon Bonaparte

**mullion** vertical piece of wood or stone between the sections of a window

**Norman** *see* Romanesque (below)

**oversailing** upper storeys of a medieval building that overhang those below

**Palladian** Classical style of building, very popular in 17th- and 18th-century Britain, following the precepts of Italian architect Andrea Palladio (1509–1580)

**pargetting** decorative plasterwork

**reredos** decorative screen behind the altar of a church

**Romanesque** pre-Gothic style of architecture of 11th and 12th centuries, also known as Norman

**rood screen/loft** medieval screen dividing the nave and chancel of a church; rare survivals have a gallery above, from which a choir would sing

**rose window** decorative circular window, with tracery lending it a flower-like appearance

**rotunda** cylindrical building

**transepts** side wings projecting north and south from the nave of a church to form the arms of a cross shape

**trilithon** doorway-shaped feature of a prehistoric monument

**tumulus** prehistoric burial mound

**vaulting/rib vaulting** raised ribs of stone supporting a roof

**fan vaulting** cone-shaped supports filled with decorative stone tracery

**weatherboarding** horizontal overlapping wooden boards forming weatherproof protection for a wall

## LANDSCAPE FEATURES

**blanket bog** bog with a grassy, shrubby surface that develops in very wet conditions

**carr woodland** woodland of water-loving trees such as willow and alder

**common** open, scrubby land where people traditionally grazed their animals

**downland** rolling, smooth hills founded on chalk

**fell** bigger than a hill, smaller than a mountain

**fen** wetland of sedge and reed

**hanger** a wood on the side of a steep slope

**limestone pavement** deeply fractured flat expanse of limestone

**machair** rich, flowery grass sward built up on shell sand

**saltings** salt marsh regularly flooded by sea tides

**sea stack** free-standing tower of sea-eroded rock

**tor** outcrop of granite, often weirdly shaped by weathering

**unimproved land** land which has never been subjected to modern farming

# INDEX

# PHOTOGRAPHIC ACKNOWLEDGEMENTS

The publishers extend their thanks to the following people
who kindly loaned their photographs
for inclusion in this book. All the photographs
in the book, with the exception of those listed below,
were supplied by Swift Imagery (John Mottershaw,
Graham Jennings, Chris Wormald, Dermot Guy-Moore,
Dennis Hardley, Tony Hyde, Dorothy Burrows, Nigel Hole,
Dr Tony Mills, Mike Morton, John Davies, Simon Clark,
Dave Saunders, Gary Lambert, Angela Rowe,
Derek Littlewood, Kevin Stockwell, Graham Swanson,
Derek Gale, David Walker, David Young, Mark Flowers,
Pearl Bucknall, Roger Howard, Roy Westlake,
Brian Hoffman, Lyndon Beddoe, Trevor Lucas, Mike Reid,
Brian Gibbs, Stephen Saffin, Neil Morris, Sue Anderson,
Chris Millington, Lawrence Englesberg, Irene Boston,
Anthony Baggett, Stephen Norris, Robert Eames,
Julian Worker, Frank Gainey, Les Norman, Helen
Harrison, John Mole, Bea Cowan, Chris Linnett, John Cox,
David Toase, Ian Booth, Graham Peacock, Linda Lane,
John Smith, Adam Swaine, Roger Hammond,
Ian Simpson, Margaret Weller, Rob Flemming):


David Cottridge: p17; p89(tr); p95(br); p121(b); p125(t)

www.britain on view.com: p26; p38; p41(b); p44(l); p60;
p66–7(c); p70; p79; p96(b); p101(t); p107; p108(r);
p118; p128-9; p132(b)

Derek Budd/Camera Ways Ltd.: p19(b); p28(b); p96(t)


t = top; b = bottom; c = centre; l = left; r = right